Chapter Five
Bristol Channel Cutter 28

She's a Modern, Old-Fashioned Beauty

The Bristol Channel Cutter (BCC) is a boat of superlatives. For many dedicated long-distance cruisers, she is, for her size, simply the best of the everything: the most comfortable, the most seaworthy, the most traditional, and (naturally) the most expensive.

There are some who call the BCC the Rolls Royce of yachts, but they've got it the wrong way around. The Rolls Royce is actually the BCC of automobiles.

What is intriguing about this boat, and the cult that has sprung up around her, is that her design is that of an old-fashioned British working boat. A century ago, scores of long-keeled cutters like her were hanging around the western approaches to the English Channel and the Irish Sea, waiting to transfer pilots to inward-bound sailing ships.

These pilot cutters needed several characteristics to survive. They had to be utterly seaworthy because they stayed out in all weathers. Gales were just an ordinary part of their working lives. They had to heave to well, because they spent much of their time waiting in one spot. But they also needed a fair turn of speed and weatherliness when a ship seeking a pilot appeared on the horizon, because it often happened that the first pilot cutter on the scene got the piloting job. And the pilots naturally favored the faster cutters.

So the design of the pilot cutters evolved as they competed to make a living at sea, being shaped by the unforgiving forces of nature and the unremitting demands of free commerce.

Not that you'd equate today's BCC with the rough-hewn finish of the working boats. The BCC, as designed by the legendary Lyle Hess and built today by the meticulous Sam Morse company, is as cultured a piece of sailing machinery as you're likely to find anywhere. In fact, you wouldn't be far wrong if you said that Chippendale and Hepplewhite were the BCCs of fine furniture.

Basic Design

Leaving the superlatives behind for a moment, what we have here is a very heavy displacement hull with moderate sail area, an outboard rudder, a long, fairly shallow keel, and a 6-foot bowsprit that certainly won't be everybody's cup of tea. It's not a recipe for daysailing or fast around-the-buoys racing.

BCC owners, who seem to have all the answers ready, will tell you a bowsprit adds sail area that spreads fore and aft, rather than upward. Thus, because it lacks the leverage of a tall skinny rig, a jib set from a sprit provides thrust without making the boat heel.

Not everybody buys that argument, suspecting that a large low sail creates exactly the same heeling moment as a small high sail; and suspecting, further, that a bowsprit was the only way you could add sail area in the days of gaff rigs, when masts had to be short because of the problems of staying them. With modern materials we can now stay tall masts quite adequately, and we can provide boats with all the sail area they need, a lot of it up high to catch more wind in light airs. We can also balance a boat very nicely without the help of a bowsprit, which means we don't have to make those daring trips to the end of the sprit to free the roller furler when the line jams.

Nevertheless, the BCC is a very safe boat to sail, even for a singlehander. You can run into a large balk of waterlogged timber on a dark night and not have to worry about bashing in a fin keel or ripping off a skeg and rudder. The BCC will ride up and over it. In shallow waters, she won't get crab-pot lines jammed in her propeller or rudder, either.

Her fairly shallow draft of 4 feet 10 inches allows her to explore the wonderful cruising grounds of the Bahamas and many other similar areas that can be tricky for those with 6-foot keels.

She is so solidly built and so well designed for her purpose that there are no modifications you need to make to improve her seaworthiness, or her fitness for ocean voyaging. There is plenty you can do personalize her, of course – in fact, if you buy a new one, starting at about $150,000, you can customer-order many modifications – but basically she's ready for sea work from the very start.

The hull is solid fiberglass, and the deck is fiberglass with a core of marine plywood. The lead keel, accounting for about 32 percent of the boat's total displacement, is encapsulated in the hull, and the double-spreader aluminum mast is stepped directly onto it.

The BCC's wide side decks are bounded by 8-inch-high teak bulwarks that provide good footing in bad weather and stop a lot of gear from disappearing over the side.

Her rudder is attached to the end of the keel and the flat transom – a strong and very sensible arrangement– and is controlled by a tiller.

Accommodations

The Sam L. Morse company builds the BCC with three basic interior layouts, and new owners are offered many options without extra charge. You can have a workbench up forward, for example, instead of a single berth. There's also the option of a pilot berth that converts into a double, and a quarterberth on the starboard side. But it's the well-planned galley that excites most comment from visitors, particularly the large amount of counter space. There probably isn't another 28-footer with a galley so pleasant to work in. But then, considering what you're paying for this boat, it darned well should be.

In Short
Bristol Channel Cutter

Designer: Lyle Hess

LOA: (including sprits): 37 feet 9 inches

LOD: 28 feet 0 inches

LWL: 26 feet 3 inches

Beam: 10 feet 1 inch

Draft: 4 feet 10 inches

Displacement: 14,000 pounds

Sail area: 556 square feet

Ballast: 4,600 pounds

Spars: Aluminum

Auxiliary: 27-hp diesel

Designed as: Bluewater cruiser

Bristol Channel
Cutter 28

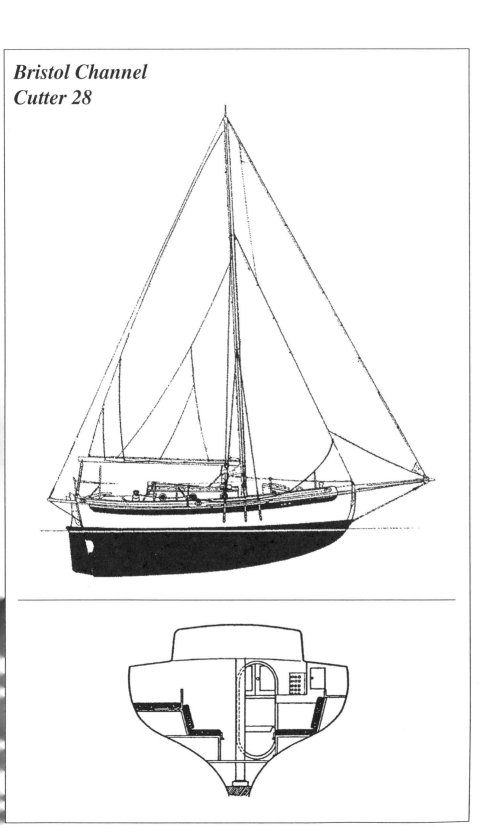

There's plenty of headroom in the main cabin – up to 6 feet 6 inches if you need it – and the cabin is unlined. That means you can get to important stuff such as plumbing and wiring – or a hole in the hull – when you need to. The raised scuttle hatch up forward provides headroom in the toilet compartment. The standard auxiliary is a 27-hp diesel, which fits into the BCC's engine hole with a comforting amount of room to spare. In general, the interior of the BCC exudes the same air of elegance and workmanship as a 1920s Pullman car, with bronze ports, a teak skylight, and lots of shippy brass.

The Rig

A gaff rig would make a lot of sense on this boat, particularly when she's sailing off the wind, which would be most of the time on an ocean cruise, presumably. It's a sturdy, well-stayed, powerful rig, one that's much more likely than a Bermuda rig to remain standing after a roll-over.

No doubt you could arrange with the Samuel L. Morse company to take delivery of a new one with a gaff rig, but the standard boat comes with a tall rig, a long bowsprit, a long boom, and a short boomkin to support the backstay clear of the mainsail leech. The mast rises 41 feet 6 inches above water level to support the 556 square feet of canvas this heavy displacement hull requires. The cutter rig is not quite as efficient to windward as a sloop rig would be – two small headsails rarely produce the same horsepower as one big one – but it certainly makes life easier for small crews.

The jib flown from the end of the bowsprit can be on a roller furler, which means it can be put to sleep as the wind pipes up, leaving a nice snug forestaysail set inboard, where it's safer to work with.

With jiffy reefing on the mainsail, and a nice flat, stable platform at the foot of the mast for you to stand on, reducing sail in a blow should be easy.

If you opt not to have a roller furling jib, you can fly an enormous genoa, Yankee, or nylon drifter from the bowsprit end, just as the Pardeys do aboard the engineless, 29-foot *Taleisin*, a close relative of the BCC. (Lin and Larry Pardey, authors of 10 sailing books, have been cruising the world for more than 30 years and have the equivalent of five circumnavigations under their keel. Their present boat, *Taleisin*, was also designed by Lyle Hess. She is slightly larger than a BCC, has a fuller bow at deck level, and has finer lines aft, with a smaller transom.)

You might not expect old-fashioned boats like the BCC to sail to windward particularly well, but sometimes they can surprise you. In the first place, their sheer mass and seakindly motion keep them moving through choppy seas that knock lighter, more lively boats backward. And in the second place, that projecting bowsprit makes it possible to trim the jib to a narrow sheeting angle and still have the sheet run outside the shrouds. So there are times when boats of this type will point surprisingly high and go surprisingly fast, which is a very handy attribute when you're faced with a two-week windward slog against the trades. But then, as we saw earlier, perhaps it's not so surprising, considering that in the last century their livelihood depended on their being able to get a pilot to windward quicker than their rivals could.

There's not much more to be said about the rig, except that it is massively solid and more than fit for the job, just like practically everything else on the boat.

Performance

The BCC does not have a kittenish performance around the buoys, but if you point her nose across an ocean you'll soon discover that she's no slouch.

"The boat can easily make 150 miles a day in the trades with the working sails only," says one owner, quoted in the advertising literature the builder puts out. "I have made many 170-mile days, and some slightly higher.

You have to accept this with due allowance for unbridled enthusiasm, of course. In theory, a boat with a waterline of 26 feet 3 inches, could do no more than 165 miles a day, at a constant speed of just over 6.8 knots. In practice, it is possible to exceed that speed in short spurts when running down the face of a wave. But even so, 165 miles in a day is very good going indeed for a non-planing boat of this size.

But perhaps the rules of physics do not apply to the BCC. Here's a part of a letter to the builder from the owner of a BCC called *Puffin*.

"Just a note to tell you *Puffin* has finally outdone herself with a 187-mile day on the way to New Zealand from Tongatapu. A good deal of near-gale-force winds and a pinch of current has pushed us 579 sea miles in four days. It looks like 1,036 sea miles in seven days, light to light."

Puffin would have had to *average* more than 7.7 knots to cover 187 miles in 24 hours. One suspects that she had more than a pinch of help from the current. The other times and distances indicate a speed of just over 6 knots, which is more reasonable.

But all quibbling aside, Lyle Hess's sturdy little cutter is obviously capable of reaching her maximum speed fairly easily– and that, in the end, is the design magic that makes a boat a swift passagemaker.

Known Weaknesses

The BCC's weaknesses are either non-existent or well hidden. One certainly never hears owners complaining about them. As befits a loyal clan of cultists, they are remarkably tight-lipped about her flaws – if, indeed, she has any. Those of us made sufficiently skeptical by practical experience will conclude that she does have flaws, but that they are remarkably minor.

There is that bowsprit, though. It's not a weakness as such, but it can be a nuisance, especially when you're docking, or playing with the jib at the splashy end of it. There's nothing you can do about it. You just have to learn to love it.

Owner's Opinions

Chris Edwards, who raced yachts to their limit for much of his sailing career, eventually graduated to a BCC. After competing in two Whitbread Round-the-World races, three Admiral's Cup races, two World One-Ton Cup championships, and so forth, Edwards found himself racing his Bristol Channel Cutter, *Xiphias*, in the inaugural series of races known as the Phuket-Port Blair Andaman Cup Regatta.

In Comparison

- Safety-at-sea factor: 1 (Rated against the 19 other boats in this book, with 1 being safest.)
- Speed rating: Good speed over long distances, from long waterline.
- Ocean comfort level: Two adults in comfort; two adults and two kids in less comfort; four adults in relative discomfort.

There were five races. The first was 450 miles across the Andaman Sea, from Phuket, Thailand to Port Blair, in India's Andaman Islands. Then there were four races of about 35 miles each among the islands.

Xiphias won the long-distance race easily on handicap – but she also beat three yachts of 34 feet, 36 feet, and 38 feet over the line. She then went on to win three of the four inshore races.

All very well, you say, but this was Chris Edwards. He could have sailed *anything* and won. Maybe. But Edwards himself says there was very little in the way of tactics involved in the ocean race. "It was a close reach on one tack for most of the race to Port Blair. It was *Xiphias's* powerful sail plan and her constant, seakindly motion in the rough seas that won the day."

He has grounded her "a couple of times," and had to contend with "some fearful tropical storms." He also says he's had to sail her hard to windward to clear a shoal or lee shore.

He says in a letter to the Samuel L. Morse company: "Her strength, her perfect balance and seakindliness, and her ability to make headway under a variety of sail settings, has convinced me that not only is she the perfect cruising design, but also a trustworthy friend."

These, of course, are obviously the sentiments of a man smitten with passion for his BCC, and you should make due allowance for it. The problem is that Chris Edwards is not alone. The files of the Samuel L. Morse company are bulging with similar letters from love-lorn owners, praising the ability of their BCCs to weather storms and look after their crews in atrocious conditions. For a common old working boat, the BCC has come a mighty long way.

Conclusion

It's tempting to note that if you have to ask the price of a Bristol Channel Cutter, you probably can't afford one. Let's just say that while they cost as much as many a small house on a modest plot of land, they'll give you a lot more in the way of adventure and excitement, if that's what you're looking for.

Chapter Six
The Cal 20

A Pocket Cruiser That Also Suits the Pocket

One has to wonder why that extraordinary adventurer Webb Chiles chose an open 18-footer like the Drascombe Lugger to sail single-handed three-quarters of the way around the world when he could have done it more safely, in far more comfort, and more cheaply in a used Cal 20.

The Cal 20 is essentially a dinghy with a lid on. She handles like a dinghy; she's light on the helm and very responsive. But she has a heavy ballast keel that makes her very stiff and safe at sea, and her cockpit is self-bailing.

She's sparsely appointed down below, to say the least, but she does have four bunks – two of which are 6 feet 6 inches long – and the cabin provides a dry, sheltered, comfortable place to sleep. That's a big step up from a Drascombe Lugger.

Better yet, the Cal 20 is cheap. Nearly 2,000 of them were built by Jensen Marine, of Costa Mesa, California, between 1961 and 1974, and the vast majority are still going strong. Some are going stronger than others, of course, but you should be able to buy a Cal 20 in excellent condition for $4,000 or $5,000 and a fixer-upper for about $2,000. Parts are still available, and racing fleets are still active on the West Coast, in the Great Lakes, and in Hawaii.

You'd have to be young and carefree to sail around the world in a Cal 20, but you wouldn't have to be foolhardy. Although she's basically a club racer/cruiser designed for nothing more than short coastal trips, she doesn't need major modification for long-distance voyaging.

She has earned a reputation for seaworthiness that is the envy of the owners of many larger, more expensive craft. George Cadwalader and his crew, Duncan Spencer, crossed the North Atlantic in one, sailing from Newport, Rhode Island, to Crookhaven, Ireland. Kun Poi Chin sailed his Cal 20, *Chalupa*, from San Francisco to Hawaii in the early 1980s.

The one thing she doesn't have is room. She is the pocket they were talking about when they invented the phrase "pocket cruiser." It's the little pocket in front of your jeans, the one that fills up with pennies, fluff, and paper clips.

Like many other boats of her size, she's little more than a floating fiberglass pup tent – except that if you're willing to put up with a little discomfort, the Cal 20 has the thrilling ability to whisk you away over the blue oceans to magical tropical islands and palm-fringed beaches.

Basic Design

One of the wonderful things about a small boat like the Cal 20 is that everything is so manageable. The sails are small, the anchor is light, and you can anti-foul the bottom in an hour. You never seem to suffer from that dreadful feeling that creeps up on you sometimes in bigger boats, that everything is just too overwhelming.

C. William ("Bill") Lapworth designed her specifically for sailors moving up from Lightnings and small dinghies. She had to be agile, like a dinghy, but she had to be big enough for weekend cruising for a couple, and possibly two small kids as well. She also had to be fast enough for weekend racing, so Lapworth stuck a 900-pound, bulb-style, ballast keel on the bottom, much like that on the Star Class. It's made of cast iron.

Her overhangs are commendably short, which gives her the most interior room possible for her length, and her accommodations also benefit from the raised foredeck, a very sensible idea that adds strength to the hull/deck unit. It's tricky to design a raised foredeck that looks right and doesn't destroy the pretty line of the sheer, but Bill Lapworth managed it very well here. Her hull is solid GRP with no coring, but the deck is of composite construction and has a plywood core, which means problems of rot and delamination if water ever manages to seep in around a poorly caulked deck fitting.

> ### *In Short*
> #### Cal 20
> Designer: C. William
>   Lapworth (1961)
> LOA: 20 feet 0 inches
> LWL: 18 feet 0 inches
> Beam: 7 feet 0 inches
> Draft: 3 feet 4 inches
> Displacement: 1,950
>   pounds
> Sail area: 196 square feet
> Ballast: 900-pound cast-
>   iron bulb
> Spars: Aluminum
> Auxiliary: 6-hp outboard
> Designed as: Daysailer,
>   racer, coastal cruiser

The Cal 20's rudder, hanging dinghy-style from the transom on pintles and gudgeons, is about as rudimentary as they come, but its simplicity and accessibility would be strong factors in its favor if repairs were ever needed. In fact, it's one of the few rudders you could remove, repair, and replace at sea.

She has a daysailer cockpit, though, an 8-foot-long affair that seats four in comfort for short periods. Its volume needs to be reduced for ocean voyaging and there are several ways to do this reasonably easily. You could, for example, make the well narrower with plywood panels. You might also use plywood to form a box at one end or the other, and gain more stowage area at the same time. But one of the best solutions was discovered by Kun Poi Chin, who simply stored his life raft in the cockpit. That reduced its volume by about 40 percent.

The cockpit coamings, incidentally, are uncomfortable to lean against. They are too low to provide good support for your back. But few problems are insoluble, it seems. If your boat has lifelines, a roller cushion fitted around the stainless steel wire could be the answer. Some owners have increased the comfort level by fitting stainless steel side railings to rest their upper bodies against.

At the aft end of the cockpit, a well for an outboard motor protrudes up for a couple of inches from the sole, sealed top and bottom with removable hatches. If you remove the hatches, you have a hole in the bottom of the boat that is less than hydrodynamically perfect. It creates swirls and eddies that slow the boat down. It also

Cal 20

35

allows water to slop into the cockpit in rough following seas. But, at the same time, it forms a huge and really efficient cockpit drain.

If you're going deepsea with this little boat, you might want to do exactly what Kun Poi Chin did. He left the bottom of the well open, but drilled holes in the top hatch and placed it back on. This stopped most of the slop splashing into the cockpit, and still acted as a drain that Chin regarded as very efficient. The standard outboard is a 6-hp model and probably the most convenient place for it, if you're going to use the well as a permanent drain in this fashion, is on the transom. In fact, however, the boat is so small that you can sail her almost anywhere, and a pair of 8-foot oars will move you around the marina or anchorage.

Accommodations

To maintain her speed and nippy performance she had to be kept light, so practically no furniture was built into the fiberglass cave below, apart from a V-berth up forward and two settee berths. Shelves and storage compartments sit at the head of the settee berths, just enough place for a camp stove on one side and a bread board on the other. There's a head compartment aft of the V-berths, big enough for a pump-through toilet. But finding space for the legally required holding tank is such a problem that most owners will opt for a portable potty, or the bucket-and-chuck-it system – alternatively, the bucket-and-bag-it system in port. Like any boat of its size and shape, the Cal 20 does not aspire to the luxury of a well to collect bilge water and keep it away from everything else in the cabin. Any water that finds its way aboard will slosh to and fro across the sole and if it isn't removed quickly, everything down below will soon be sodden. This means that clothes and important documents should be kept in watertight containers, just in case.

The original boats were supplied with a flush-through toilet between the berths in the forepeak. But current legislation calls for holding tanks to be fitted to fixed toilets, and there is simply no space for a tank of any reasonable size in a Cal 20. So most owners have thrown out the original toilet and replaced it with a portable toilet. This allows them to glass over the two through-hulls the original toilet needed and reduce the number of holes in the hull.

The Rig

You could hardly design a simpler rig than this. The Cal 20 is a sloop with 196 square feet of sail area, a Bermudian mainsail and a 7/8th foretriangle to hang the jib from. No great strains here; but remember this is a small boat and a third row of reef points in the mainsail is a good idea for offshore work. The spars are anodized aluminum.

The standard stays and shrouds were designed for daysailing. If you're taking a Cal 20 to sea you should replace them with ones at least a size bigger all around. Incidentally, be sure to check out the original spreader brackets for cracks or other signs of deterioration. They're the weakest part of the rig, according to Steve Seal, an Alameda, California, sparmaker and supplier of rigging parts for several makes of sailboats. He carries spare parts for the Cal 20. You'll find his page on the Internet if you search for Seal's Spars and Rigging.

Performance

With 46 percent of her nominal displacement low down on her keel, the Cal 20 is a stiff little boat. In fact she has built a reputation in San Francisco for being able to carry full working sail downwind in 30 knots.

Her stiffness means she works to windward at a minimal angle of heel, which is less tiring on the crew but harder on the rigging – hence the need to upgrade the stays and shrouds for ocean work.

She's no flier, of course. She couldn't be, with only 18 feet of waterline length on a full displacement hull, but she has earned a respectable PHRF rating of 264 on the Northern California PHRF list. The ubiquitous Catalina 22 with a swing keel rates 270 on the same list.

For a small boat, she's fairly dry. Her ample freeboard, combined with the raised foredeck, takes care of a lot of the spray. But dryness is comparative, of course, and no boat of this size can truly be called dry when beating to windward in the open sea in heavy weather. Nevertheless, her reputation for seaworthiness is well earned.

> ### In Comparison
> - Safety-at-sea factor: 19 (Rated against the 19 other boats in this book, with 1 being safest.)
> - Speed rating: PHRF 264. Not bad for her size and weight.
> - Ocean comfort level: No comfort whatsoever, but she can accommodate two adults with their elbows in each other's faces. A good candidate for singlehanding.

As the windspeed rises, she tends to develop some weather helm, which can be cured by reefing the mainsail and keeping the working jib flying as long as possible. When it's time to change down to a storm jib, it's also time to take in another reef in the mainsail, too. Excessive heeling in this boat is the major cause of weather helm, and sailing her more upright is the key to control, so in really heavy weather a third row of reef points for the mainsail is a good idea. Downwind, though, she really shows her stiffness, and racing Cal 20s often carry their spinnakers long after other classes have doused theirs.

Known Weaknesses

• Check the foredeck for rot of the plywood core and separation of the fiberglass layers, inside and outside, from the core. Water seeping into the plywood over the years will eventually soften the plywood and cause delamination. It's not easy to fix.

• The original spreader brackets have been known to crack.

• Excessive lee helm or weather helm is sometimes caused by a badly cast or slightly misaligned keel. Some owners have gone to the trouble of fairing out the keel to improve its performance; and re-aligning the keel is not a big job, but it's one you would rather not have to do in the first place.

• Some boats that have been raced hard have managed to loosen the deck attachment points for the forestay and the aft lower shrouds. Check them carefully and beef them up if necessary.

Owner's Opinion

If you're planning to cross an ocean in a Cal 20, you'd do well to contact *Cruising*

World magazine in Newport, Rhode Island (401) 847-1588 – and ask for a copy of an article called "Expand Your Pocket Cruiser's Horizons," by Kun Poi Chin. It appeared in the September, 1985, issue. Your local library may also be able to help you locate the article.

As we've already mentioned, Chin sailed his Cal 20, *Chalupa*, from San Francisco to Hawaii in the early 1980s. He weathered six days and nights of gales during the 20-day trip, and went on to cruise more than 1,000 miles among the Hawaiian islands without major problems.

He did, however, beef up the original hull before he left. For a start, he glassed in a full-length internal stringer of wood and foam from bow to stern on either side of the hull. He replaced the portlights with 1/8-inch Lexan and through-bolted them. He stiffened the bulkhead under the mast and installed new keel bolts with extra-large washers. He also replaced the rudder with a stronger one with heftier pintles and gudgeons, and he anchored the aft lower shrouds and the forestay more securely.

Chin carried no engine. He relied for auxiliary power on a pair of 8-foot oars.

He summarized his Cal 20 adventure this way: "Taking a small boat designed for coastal sailing on the ocean required some compromises. I accepted that. But after a year of cruising, I do not think that I could find another boat of the same size that would provide me with all the fun and joy of cruising at such an affordable price."

Voyaging in small craft, he added, might not be for everyone, but if you want to do it badly enough, it's definitely possible. And the key is simple: "An attitude of how little one needs, rather than how much wants, is required."

Conclusion

Kun Poi Chin pretty much said it all. If you're adventurous and filled with a passion for cruising, you can do it very cheaply in reasonable safety with a bit of planning and a lot of caution. You can do it in a Cal 20. Voyaging in a boat as small as this comes at the expense of physical comfort, of course, and it requires commonsense planning of your route. But the rewards are great. The experience will breed confidence, independence, and abilities that will serve you well for the rest of your life.

Chapter Seven
Cape Dory 25D

Unique Interior for a Classy Classic

The important thing to remember about this boat is the "D" behind her name. There are about 26 different kinds of Cape Dory yachts, both power and sail, ranging from the original Cape Dory 10 to the Cape Dory 45. There are, in addition, two Cape Dory 25s, but only one is the Cape Dory 25D. And she is quite different from the Cape Dory 25 without the "D" – which, incidentally, stands for "diesel."

The very name Cape Dory conjures up images of traditional designs, high-quality building, and extraordinary customer loyalty. In short, the 25D is a cult boat, with active owners' associations, a site on the Worldwide Web, and high resale value. That should be "comparatively high resale value," of course, because as ocean cruisers go, the 25D is not expensive. On the East or Gulf Coasts, where most of them are, you can expect to pay between $12,000 and $15,000 for one.

She is a pedigreed design – an Alberg, like almost all the Cape Dory line – but she doesn't have the usual skinny hull of his older boats. She has a beam of 8 feet on a waterline of 19 feet, a reasonably generous modern proportion, and it shows in her interior. Down below, she is probably one of the most functional mini-cruisers ever designed for two people.

She is in no way an updated Cape Dory 25, which was designed by George Stadel and originally produced by Allied as the Greenwich 24. Andrew Vavolotis, owner of Cape Dory Yachts, bought the tooling and redesigned the boat, relaunching her as the Cape Dory 25 in 1973.

And then, in the fall of 1981, the Cape Dory 25D came along, sowing great confusion everywhere. She was also a Cape Dory, and she was also 25 feet long, but she was wider, heavier, deeper, and derived auxiliary power from a small inboard diesel instead of a gasoline outboard.

The 25D has been compared with the classic 25-foot British design, the Vertue. Numbers of this Laurent Giles favorite are found all over the world, and many have made circumnavigations. In theory, even though the 25D is about half the displacement of a Vertue, she's equally capable of deepsea work; but for some reason she has not yet developed the same kind of reputation. Perhaps her time is yet to come.

Basic Design

She has a solid GRP hull, but her decks and the cabintop are GRP/balsa sandwiches. End-grain balsa is extremely light, and it's highly resistant to crushing. It also provides good insulation against heat, cold, and sound. But it has a wicked habit of soaking up water and turning to slush if you don't take a lot of trouble to seal the through-holes for deck fittings.

Luckily, balsa that has deteriorated is usually quite easy to detect, either by tapping the deck with a screwdriver handle and listening for a dull thud instead of a good solid ring, or else simply by jumping up and down on it heavily.

The 25D has an old-fashioned, hard-bilged, full keel – a true sea-going keel, slightly cut away up forward – and a deep-displacement hull. Her rudder has a straight after edge and is squared off at the bottom. It hangs off the end of the keel, with the rudder stock appearing well aft in the cockpit. The propeller spins in an aperture cut half from the rudder and half from the deadwood. This is a real cruising underbody, strong and very resistant to tangling with crabbers' underwater lines.

Above the waterline she looks solidly and pleasingly traditional, although her mast is taller and her sailplan more efficient than those of most traditional boats. Her cabin house has the chunky, purposeful appearance of a boat that works for its living, yet it avoids looking boxy. Her cocky sheerline manages well the important task of resolving the aesthetic conflict between a straight, sawn-off counter stern and a rounded bow with a moderate overhang.

The cockpit is generously sized – in fact it's bordering on too large for serious ocean work – but it does have a sensible bridgedeck to prevent water cascading down below in the event of a pooping. There is a shallow cockpit locker to starboard and a deeper one to port.

An anchor roller is built into the stemhead forestay fitting, and the foredeck also accommodates a reasonably-sized anchor locker capable of holding an anchor, some chain, and a normal nylon rode. In general, the foredeck is free of toe-stubbing fittings and feels bigger than it really is.

The standard engine is the little 7 1/2-hp Yanmar diesel, a neat installation that weighs little more than 150 pounds. It's cooled by raw sea water and drives a two-bladed bronze propeller. The 25D's nominal range under power at cruising speed is about 200 to 250 miles, drawing about a quart of fuel an hour from her 13-gallon tank. Access to the engine is pretty good, via a lift-out bin in the top of the covering box, and also – if you need to get really up close and serious – by taking away the companionway steps and the front panel of the box.

Accommodations

As far as the accommodations of the 25D go, Carl Alberg did a very sensible thing by putting the head where the V-berth would normally be. By opting to do without a cramped V-berth, he opened up a large toilet and storage area capable of being closed off completely from the rest of the boat – a real luxury in a 25-footer.

This arrangement makes a great deal of sense for a cruising couple, for whom a V-berth would just be a place to store random odds and ends such as blown-out sails and expired flares anyway. There are two settee berths in the main cabin, a short-looking one to port whose foot-locker protrudes through the main bulkhead to form a countertop in the head compartment, and a normal-looking one to starboard that pulls out to form a double. There's also a fourth bunk if anyone should need it, a quarterberth to starboard.

Cape Dory 25D

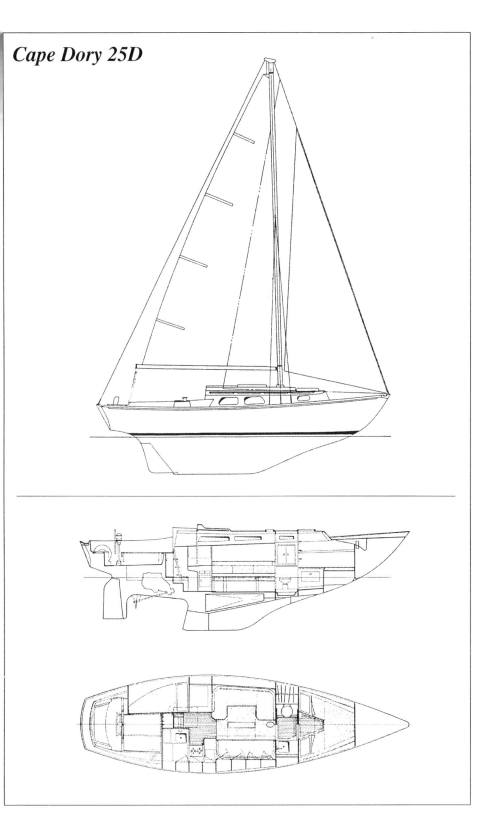

A cabin sole located low in the bilge provides standing headroom throughout the boat – 5 feet 11 inches in the saloon and 5 feet 9 inches in the head compartment, which has its own deck-opening hatch and two opening ports for ventilation.

Unfortunately, there's a design law that says if you stick four full-sized bunks and an oversized head into a 25-footer, you don't have any room left over for a chart table, and precious little for a galley. There is a galley, to be sure, but it would delight only the heart of a Spartan. It features a twin-burner alcohol stove, which produces little heat at great expense, and a stainless steel sink whose main feature seems to be inaccessibility. It is largely hidden beneath the bridgedeck and its freshwater pump is so artfully concealed and difficult to work that it might have been conceived deliberately to save water. In fact, bachelor sailors might be tempted to wash their dishes in the head, where there's a sink right out in the open where you can reach it, but for more fastidious crews, washing up on this boat will mean sitting in the cockpit with a bucket. Still, all in all, it's not a bad swap for such a comfortable sleeping cabin and head compartment. And if you're handy with tools, the galley situation could be improved fairly easily. The ports in the main cabin all open to provide wonderful cross-breezes in hot climates, and almost certainly the odd drip of rainwater in more temperate climates. They are solid bronze and add greatly to the 25D's air of old-fashioned reliability.

The Rig

The 25D carries a comparatively tall mast, stepped on deck but supported underneath by a compression post that takes the load straight to the keel. This avoids the very common problem of deck beams and bulkheads buckling under the constant downward pressure exerted by the mast.

The masthead sloop rig is simple, efficient, and easily managed. The mainsail has an area of 140 square feet and the foretriangle measures 164 square feet, making cockpit sheet winches more of a cruising convenience than a necessity. The mainsheet traveler is sensibly located aft of the tiller.

Double lower shrouds support the mast at each side, and a single forestay and backstay running to the truck take care of fore-and-aft movement.

The shrouds terminate at their lower ends in massive chainplates set into the hull/deck joint, and while that interferes with the sheeting angle of the jib, it provides the widest – and therefore most stable – base of support for the mast. That's an important consideration with a high-aspect-ratio rig.

Performance

Her hard bilges and high ballast ratio make her quite stiff, and she stands up to her canvas well but, as in any small boat, you'll need to reef her mainsail when the wind gets up to around 16 or 20 knots. She is modern enough (just) to have come equipped with efficient jiffy reefing instead of the troublesome main-boom roller reefing so favored by builders in earlier years.

She's no racer, but her PHRF rating of 252 proves she's no sluggard, either. She'll need a bit of help in calm weather to overcome the frictional resistance of her large underwater area, though, and large light foresails will provide it.

You'll find the shrouds prevent you from sheeting in a 100-percent foresail tight enough for really high pointing, but if you're willing to go to the trouble of re-arranging the sheeting, you can bring the foresail sheet inboard of the shrouds for a beat, making use of a length of track on the cabintop, and take it back outside the shrouds for a reach or a run.

If you're beating in any kind of chop, you probably won't bother to change the sheeting position because you'll need to fall off the wind a little, in any case, to gain enough power to drive you through the waves.

Known Weaknesses

• Poor access to the galley sink. See under Accommodations above.

• Water capacity. She carries only 20 gallons of drinking water in a plastic tank. For an ocean crossing, you'd need to double that amount at least, carrying the extra in small cans or a flexible bladder.

• No chart table. It's not an unusual failing, even in much larger boats, but the appointments of the 25D seem so solid and complete that you notice it more here. A cunningly placed sheet of plywood, or a folding table, would suffice.

Owners' Opinions

Bob Ohler sails his Cape Dory 25D, *Aloha Spirit*, hull #2, out of Deale, Maryland, and cruises in the Middle Chesapeake. He has been sailing for 20 years and does a lot of singlehanding. He says the 25D is ideal for that. In his part of the world they talk about "Cape Dory days." That's when the wind is in the northwest, blowing 18 to 22 knots, and the bay is covered with whitecaps. The boat loves it.

The first thing he does when the wind starts to rise is take one reef in the mainsail. That happens at about 16 knots. "She's well balanced and very easy to control then," he says. "My wife never has any trouble with her. The boat has a little weather helm, but that's a good thing and it never gets excessive if you reef in time."

He finds the boat good and stiff. In fact he has sailed her in 30 knots and 5-foot seas with a working foresail and just one reef in the main. It's not the sort of thing he'd recommend for long, especially at sea, but it shows the boat can take it.

He raked the mast back 6 degrees to make her point better, and when he's going to windward he uses the Cunningham cringle for a flattening reef. "It makes her point 10 degrees higher," he claims.

She needs some sort of headsail at all times," he notes. "It seems to help to windward, especially – prevents her hobbyhorsing and plugging away in the same hole. She'll do that if you don't have a jib to pull her over the waves." He says she's also a star performer on a reach under foresail only.

Aloha Spirit has a Yanmar 1GM single-cylinder, 7-hp diesel, which Ohler cautiously describes as "adequate." He always wears a safety harness when he's alone and strings jacklines of 1-inch nylon webbing from

In Short
Cape Dory 25D

Designer: Carl Alberg (1981)

LOA: 25 feet 0 inches

LWL: 19 feet 0 inches

Beam: 8 feet 0 inch

Draft: 3 feet 6 inches

Displacement: 5,120 pounds

Sail area: 304 square feet

Ballast: Encapsulated lead

Spars: Aluminum

Auxiliary: 7 1/2 hp diesel

Designed as: Conservative cruiser

the bow, around each side of the cabintop, and back to the cockpit.

His headsail has a downhaul that leads back to cockpit, just as the foresail halyard does, so he can drop the sail at will. Then he trims and cleats the sheet to keep the sail firmly in place on deck.

He's against roller furling on the foresail. "I've had it on other boats," he says. "You just never know when it will go wrong. I'd never go back to it."

For deepsea work, he advises that you:
• Check the chainplates for rust.
• Get a solar panel to keep the batteries charged.
• Fit a self-steering wind vane.

Mike Smith sails his Cape Dory 25D, *Solitude*, out of Niantic, Connecticut. He has owned her since 1986 and put in a lot of hours in all kinds of weather up and down the coast. *Solitude* has a 135-percent genoa on a roller furler gear, so the first thing Smith does when the wind pipes up is crank in the jib.

At about 16 to 20 knots, the jib will need to be down to about 100 percent, and he'll take in the first of the two jiffy reefs he has in the mainsail.

"She gets weather helm as she heels over," Smith says, "but as soon as you take that reef in the main and flatten out the sail, she's perfect – easy to handle.

He finds the boat the ideal size for singlehanding, although she's also comfortable with two aboard. "She's not a handful," he notes. "Everything is set up nicely in the cockpit for a singlehander. Even docking is not problem.

He, too, has the standard Yanmar 7-hp diesel, but has stronger views about it, perhaps because *Solitude* often needs a very strong push upriver against the tide. "It's grossly underpowered," he feels. "I'd like to replace it with a 12-horse, two-cylinder diesel in a couple of years.

His advice for anyone contemplating an ocean voyage in a 25D
• Beef up the lower shrouds. Make the standing rigging 1/4-inch diameter all around.
• Secure the companionway hatchboards in place at sea.
• Add padeyes in the cockpit for your safety harness.
• Run safety jacklines of nylon webbing or tubing from the bow cleats to the stern cleats.

In Comparison

• Safety-at-sea factor: 13 (Rated against the 19 other boats in this book, with 1 being safest.)

• Speed rating: Not fast, but not bad for an out-and-out cruiser. In the Northeast USA, her PHRF rating is 252. In comparison, a Herreshoff 28 ketch rates 255.

• Ocean comfort level: One or two adults in comfort; two adults and two kids in discomfort.

Conclusion

You'd go a long way to find a 25-foot boat with a better interior than this for serious cruising. Doing away with the V-berth up forward was a radical design concept, but a real winner in a boat dedicated from the start to cruising. For $12,000 to $15,000 (maybe a little more if she has been upgraded and maintained to meticulous standards) you can buy a classic Alberg that will take you anywhere in a lot more safety and comfort than you'll find in almost any other 25 footer you care to name.

Chapter Eight
Catalina 27

An Unlikely Round-the-Worlder

It might come as a surprise to find the Catalina 27 listed in a book of boats supposedly seaworthy enough to sail around the world. I can think of some dedicated traditionalists who would faint dead away at the very suggestion.

But she is included here for some very practical reasons. Firstly, a lot of people are going to be tempted to take the Catalina 27 offshore. They should know what her limitations are. Secondly, Catalina 27s *have* sailed around the world very successfully. Prospective adventurers need to know how that success was achieved. Thirdly, Catalina 27s are very available. They're belly-button boats. Everyone seems to have one. And they're cheap. More than 6,000 27s have been produced since Frank Butler started building them in California in 1971. It's the largest production run of a 27-foot sailboat in the history of boatbuilding.

Perhaps it's important to state the obvious right at the beginning: a good sailor could sail around the world in almost anything. Just because the Catalina 27 has made circumnavigations, it doesn't make her anything like the ideal boat. Nevertheless, her weak points are well known, and she is capable of being improved substantially by enthusiastic amateurs. She's not the kind of boat you'd want to take around Cape Horn in winter, but with a lot of caution and seamanlike preparation you could sail her around the Cape of Good Hope in summer.

Before you rush out and start looking at secondhand Catalina 27s, be aware that there are several different models, some more suitable than others for ocean work. There are models with deep keels and shoal-draft keels. Some have tall rigs, and others have standard rigs. About half have outboard engines and the rest have inboard engines. The two standard interior designs are the traditional version, with the galley located aft, and the dinette version, which has the galley amidships.

For our purposes, the deep-keel, tall-rig, aft-galley, outboard engine version is most suitable. With a tall rig, you can fly plenty of sail to get you through calms. Why an outboard? We'll come to that in a bit.

The original displacement of the deep-keel outboard model was about 5,600 pounds, while the shoal-draft 27 displaced about 6,100 pounds, the extra 500 pounds being carried as added ballast in the keel.

But as the years have rolled by, the Catalina 27 has put on weight along with the rest of us. Displacement of later boats has crept up to 6,800 pounds or more as the interior has become more sophisticated and loaded down with inboard engines and the paraphernalia of sewage holding tanks, Y-valves, fuel tanks, and so on.

An older, lighter boat is probably your best bet for an extended sea voyage. You're going to add plenty of weight in the form of food and water, and you don't want to destroy this boat's main asset – her speed and sailing ability – by burdening her too much.

Basic Design

The first thing you could say about the Catalina 27 is that she was designed to be affordable. That is, cheap. There is no expensive overbuilding here, no redundant overlapping systems, no salty bronze opening ports at more than $100 a smack. She was designed for a purpose, and she fulfills that purpose well. Let's just not kid ourselves that she was *designed* to sail around the world.

The Catalina 27 is a fin-keeler with a free-standing rudder extending aft underwater beneath the transom. There is no support from a skeg. The first thing you notice about her is that she handles like a dinghy, which is hardly surprising since that's what she basically is – a dinghy with delusions of grandeur. She's light and beamy. The tall rig is skinny and efficient. She is reasonably stiff and stands up well to her canvas. All this makes her a fast, maneuverable, and easily controlled boat, but it doesn't do much for seaworthiness.

With a beam of 8 feet 6 inches (later increased to 8 feet 10 inches) the hull needs to be fairly shallow, so as not to increase displacement and underwater resistance. That, in turn, limits the space inside for accommodations and stowage. But what the Catalina 27 lacks below the waterline is more than compensated for by what's above it. This boat is a good example of nautical trompe l'oeil. She deceives the eye. Her topsides are deep and her cabintop high, so that her interior is actually about the biggest you'll find on any boat with a 22-foot waterline. But you wouldn't think so by just looking at her from the outside. Through some cunning design, or by pure luck, Frank Butler happened on a bulky design that is not aesthetically offensive. Far from it. She's not a bad looker at all. The deep crown in the cabintop helps considerably, and the fairly straight sheerline gives her a look of modern sleekness, but there's something else at work there, too, some magic mingling of line, curve, and proportion that brings pleasure to the eye.

The decks and cockpits of older boats were what you might call uncluttered, even with essentials such as a bow roller, but that can be an advantage, too. Sometimes it's easier to start with a clean sheet and add your own custom fittings. Incidentally, in the beginning there were no backing plates on the fittings that *were* supplied; that kind of pennypinching inevitably leads to cracked gel coats and possible delamination of the GRP around the bases of stanchions, cleats, and rails. Happily, things changed for the better on later boats.

The 27's cockpit is fairly large and lacks a proper bridgedeck to stop heavy water entering the saloon. There are ways around this problem that we will discuss later, but they bring with them the usual penalties – inconvenience and the need for constant vigilance.

A little earlier we asked why an outboard engine is the type recommended for an extended voyage. The answer is simple. Although about half of all Catalina 27s are fitted with inboard engines, they shouldn't be. It's possible to squeeze one of those

Catalina 27

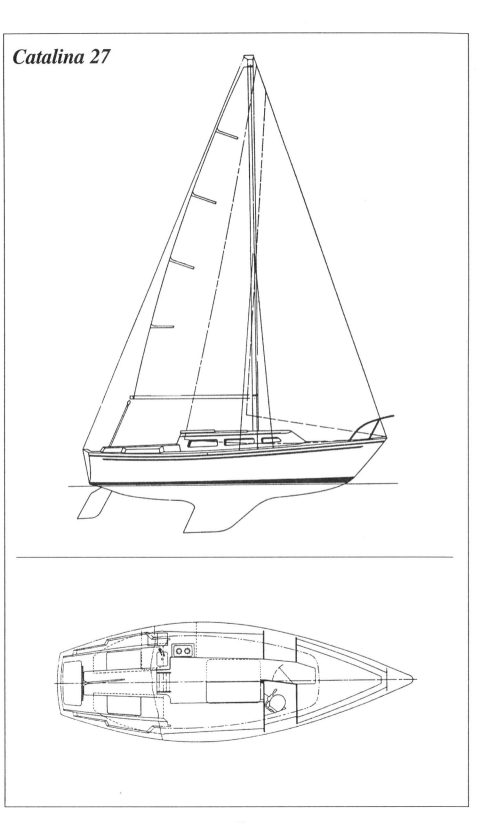

sweet-running little Universal 14-hp twins into the space aft of the saloon, and then bolt the deck and cockpit on top of it, but there's practically no way to get to it after that. You might as well kiss it goodbye.

As a result of poor access, and the consequent problems of routine servicing, the inboard engine of a used boat is likely to have been neglected unless the previous owner was double-jointed and could change the oil by feel alone.

The outboard-engine versions of the 27 free up a lot of stowage space down below and avoid most of the problems of servicing, although they're not exactly easy to manhandle in and out of the well at the aft end of the cockpit. In fact, if you're planning to cross an ocean, it would be better to mount the outboard on a bracket attached to the outer face of the transom. That frees up some valuable lazarette space.

A 9.9-hp outboard is about the right size for the Catalina 27, though you can go as low as 5 hp if you intend to motor only when there's not enough wind to sail. And then you could use the same engine on your inflatable dinghy. The Catalina 27 can't carry much gasoline, of course, so her range under power will be limited, but she sails so well that you'll only need the engine for getting through the odd pass in a coral reef, or for maneuvering in port.

Accommodations

There's hardly another 27-footer around that compares with the Catalina 27 for a feeling of bright airiness and space down below. Despite her faults, and they are many, this boat offers so much in the way of accommodations that owners are prepared to overlook the rest.

The companionway hatch is responsible for much of the spacious feeling. It's very wide. When it's fully opened, the heavens appear to invade the boat's interior, letting in light, air, and the sweet smell of the sea. At the same time, a hatch as big as that is a distinct danger at sea, not only because it is structurally weaker than a smaller one, but also because of the vast volume of water it would admit if the boat were suddenly capsized while it was open.

There is standing headroom of 6 feet 1 inch in the main cabin, but it tapers down as you move forward. Still, for a 27-footer it's very generous.

The traditional aft-galley layout supports six berths. They aren't all comfortable to sleep in – the two in the forecabin and the one on the port side of the main cabin are short – but nobody should even contemplate sleeping six adults in a Catalina 27 anyway. The settee berth on the starboard side converts into a double bed for cozy cuddling in port, but the only really decent sea bed is the starboard quarterberth.

Just aft of the forecabin, on the starboard side, there's an enclosed head that is reasonably comfortable to use.

As is usual on a boat of this size, there's precious little locker space, although many owners have found that they can open up extra stowage pockets by cutting into the plastic interior liner in strategic places.

The original galley equipment was a two-burner alcohol stove, which can be recommended only if you have plenty of time on your hands and enjoy spending a lot of money on a little heat. Propane is quicker, easier, and more efficient. It can also be dangerous. But then, so can going to sea in a Catalina 27. Traditionalists will change over to kerosene, which is smellier and messier and more trouble, but safer and cheaper.

Over the years, the Catalina 27's rather austere looks down below have been softened by the addition of more wooden trim, but its side effects are detrimental, both on the speed of the boat and the checkbook of the owner. This boat will never look like a Hinckley or a Hallberg-Rassy, no matter how much trim they add.

The Rig

The Catalina 27 is not dressed for the sea. Her rig is weak and needs to be beefed up. Shrouds and stays should be replaced with wire at least one size bigger. The chainplates for the aft lower shrouds should be strengthened, too. Owners of older boats like to tell how they watched the deck bowing upward at the chainplates in heavy weather. Some bolted new stainless steel chainplates through the topsides, as was the fashion in the good old days, and fastened the shrouds to them. It means the jib won't sheet at such a narrow angle, but it's a good trade for keeping the mast up.

Change the spreader sockets, too. The old ones were made of cast aluminum, which has a reputation of cracking under stress. You can get new stainless steel ones from the factory.

Otherwise, the rig is pretty simple and efficient – a single-spreader masthead sloop of 340 square feet, with the sail area fairly evenly divided between the main and fore triangle. The spars are aluminum, of course, and she uses jiffy reefing on the mainsail.

Performance

The tall-rig, deep-keel, outboard-engine Catalina 27 that is best suited to deep-sea work is also the best performer. The secret of making fast passages in this boat is to keep her light. She will not only sail faster and go to windward better, but she'll be safer because she'll put less strain on her hull and rigging. When she's pounded by a wave, a boat like this must be able to give way fast. She hasn't got the strength to resist like a solid rock, and take everything that comes. She must submit. Her narrow keel helps her to slip sideways through the water, and so reduce the force of the blow, but too much weight will sink her lower, slow her responses, and punish her accordingly. A Catalina 27 must be lively to live.

So be careful how you load her. Take only enough food and water for the passage in hand. Resist the temptation to stock up on canned goods for three years because your local supermarket is having the sale of a lifetime. Keep that weight down. The outboard version is faster than the inboard version for two reasons: an outboard is a fraction of the weight of an inboard engine, and you can raise an outboard's propeller out of the water to avoid drag.

Under sail she's lively but you can control her with one finger on the tiller until it really starts to blow. She

In Short

Catalina 27

Designer: Frank Butler (1971)

LOA: 26 feet 10 inches

LWL: 21 feet 9 inches

Beam: 8 feet 6 inches

Draft: 3 feet 5 inches (shoal) or 4 feet 0 inch

Displacement: 6,850 pounds

Sail area: 340 square feet

Ballast: 2,700 pounds

Spars: Aluminum

Auxiliary: Gas or diesel, inboard or outboard

Designed as: Entry-level daysailer and coastal cruiser/racer won't hold her course faithfully for 10 minutes while you clean up the mess the anchor made on the foredeck, of course, although she tracks better than you might expect from a fin keeler. The lightness of the helm is an advantage in at least one respect: you can use a small self-steering windvane such as the Navik, which weighs only 41 pounds.

Like most beamy little lightweights, she tends to gather weather helm as the wind rises and makes her heel excessively. Weather helm describes a sailboat's continuous attempt to gripe, or turn into the wind, which must be counteracted by pulling the tiller to weather.

There are ways to deal with excessive weather helm, either by varying the amount of sail fore and aft, so that she is forced to turn away from the wind by more sail area forward, or by changing the depth of draft in a sail. But the best way to reduce weather helm and maintain control on a boat like the Catalina 27 is to reef down. As soon as she comes more upright, the tendency to gripe is greatly reduced.

You can try this for yourself in the bathtub with a model yacht. If you push the mast from directly behind when she's dead upright, the yacht will go straight ahead. If you push in the same spot while she's heeled over to starboard, she'll spin around to port. The mast acts as a sideways lever to screw her into the wind. And the more she heels the more effective that lever is.

So keep your Catalina 27 upright– or at least reduce that excessive angle of heel – by reefing down as soon as you experience that feeling that she's getting out of control.

Known Weaknesses

• We've already mentioned the backing plates for deck fittings, the standing rigging, the chainplates, and the spreader sockets.

• The lack of a bridge deck means you'll have to keep one or more hatchboards in place in the companionway, and you must be sure they're solidly fixed in place so you won't lose them in a capsize. They will hamper your access to the cockpit – you will have to high-step over them every darned time you come and go – but it's a small penalty to pay for the security it provides.

• Check the seacocks. You must have a bronze seacock on every through-hull opening. Some of the original through-hull fittings on the Catalina 27 were simply pipe nipples glassed into the hull. Change them for proper flanged, bolt-through bronze through-hulls. And if your boat has gate valves fitted to the through-hulls instead of seacocks, change them, too. Gate valves, no matter what material they're made of, are not seagoing fittings. Change them for bronze ball seacocks, or the traditional tapered barrel type.

• Check the icebox drain. There have been reports of water running back into the box when the boat heels over. Fit a seacock to the through-hull.

Owner's Opinion

I once tested a Catalina 27 for a week for *Cruising World* magazine and found her quite free of vices under sail and power. I didn't have to opportunity to test her in extreme

In Comparison
• Safety-at-sea factor: 20 (Rated against the 19 other boats in this book, with 1 being safest.)
• Speed rating: Relatively fast. Average PHRF rating about 200.
• Ocean comfort level: Two adults in a small degree of comfort.

conditions at sea, but I discovered a man who did. He's Patrick Childress, of Newport, Rhode Island, who sailed his secondhand Catalina 27 *Juggernaut* around the world alone in the 1980s.

He experienced the worst weather of his trip in the cantankerous and unpredictable Indian Ocean. During a particularly bad storm he stripped *Juggernaut* down to a storm jib. He then sheeted it in tightly and set his Navik wind-vane self-steering gear to keep *Juggernaut* close on the wind.

With the boat heeled well over, even under the tiny jib, she gained weather helm, so there was not much work for the Navik to do to keep her heading about 45 degrees into the waves as she forged slowly ahead. This is a classic hove-to position, but very few classic boats ever manage to achieve it, and it's ironic that a boat normally considered unsuitable for deep-sea work should be able to heave to so well in extreme conditions.

She occasionally got lifted up by an extra-big wave and dumped down sideways, but she always recovered quickly, so Childress left her at it until the storm blew itself out.

Childress got his boat very cheaply and worked full-time for three months to make her fit for sea. Here are some of the major changes he made:

• He stiffened the hull by installing mini-bulkheads in all storage areas beneath the berths. This also divided the stowage into more conveniently sized compartments, of course.

• He installed a 1-inch-thick mahogany plank inside the starboard side of the transom as a stiffener and backing plate for an outboard engine bracket.

• He improved cockpit drainage by installing four large hoses leading downward between the aft end of the cockpit and the transom. There were through-hull fittings at each end of each pipe.

• He stopped water forcing its way through the front and sides of the closed main hatch by making new, tighter-fitting runners. He also fixed plastic tabs on the front of the hatch.

• He bolted new chainplates through the hull.

• He changed the stove burners from alcohol to kerosene. The threads are the same, so it is a simple matter of unscrewing the old burner and screwing in the new one.

• He installed double headstays.

• He fitted heavier topmast shrouds and aft lower shrouds. The forward lower shrouds stayed the same.

• He installed open-faced, stronger turnbuckles.

• He installed double backstays, with a backstay adjuster. He removed the forward bolt on the rudder bracket, the one that goes through tiller, and replaced it with two stainless steel hose clamps.

• He installed a 1/2-inch bolt through the rudder-post cap, where the cap attaches to the rudder stock. The original bolt is too small and will eventually wear an oblong hole.

• He installed a medium-duty electric bilge pump in bilge, fitted with float switch and manual override. He also installed a large capacity electric pump with a float switch in the protected area under the cockpit for extreme emergencies in case cabin became flooded. (He used to solar panel to charge his one battery, aided occasionally by a small-capacity generator on his outboard motor.)

  • He caulked the hull-deck joint with 3M-5200 sealant to fill the void behind the rubrail, which was leaking.

  • He boarded over outboard engine well and fitted his Navik self-steering gear there.

Conclusion

We live in an age when it is both fashionable and legally advisable to warn people about the many ways in which they can harm or kill themselves. One is forced to wonder how people ever managed to survive before this fashion was all the rage, how the human population of the world ever managed to grow to the record level it is at today.

So while it is correct to say that going to sea in a Catalina 27 can be harmful to your health, one always harbors the hope that anyone imbued with the human spirit of adventure and the need to explore will deem the risks necessary, even invigorating.

Of course you shouldn't go to sea in a 27 if you're an absolute beginner with no knowledge of sailing or navigation. But if you're a reasonably experienced sailor with a good deal of common sense, and are prepared to work to get the boat right, and study to make sure you're in the right places at the right seasons, there's no practical reason why you shouldn't sail an old Catalina 27 around the world, as others have before you. And a whole lot of us would cheer you on.

Chapter Nine
Contessa 26/J. J. Taylor 26

Minimum Price for Maximum Seaworthiness

The Contessa 26, also known as the J. J. Taylor 26, is one of many variations on the basic Folkboat theme, but she has several unique claims to fame. Not the least among them is the name of her designer, the British naval architect David Sadler, who also designed the Contessa 32.

You may recall that the Contessa 32 was the only yacht to finish in her class – the smallest class, incidentally – in the infamous Fastnet Race of 1979. When a particularly vicious storm hit the racing fleet between England and Ireland, five yachts sank, 19 were abandoned, and 15 lives were lost. Only 85 yachts of 303 starters crossed the finish line.

Although the Contessa 26 is far different from the Contessa 32, above the waterline and below, Sadler's ability to design safe, seaworthy boats is quite evident in the Contessa 26 as well. The 26 was also well publicized by the circumnavigations of Tania Aebi and Brian Caldwell, of course. Aebi became the youngest woman to sail around the world alone in *Varuna* – although she was technically disqualified for sailing one short leg with a companion. Later, Brian Caldwell chose a bright red 1975 Contessa 26 called Mai (Miti) Vavau – "Waves from a Distant Storm"– for his attempt to become the youngest person to sail around the world alone.

From the very first, the 26 gained a reputation for seaworthiness combined with good performance. Many of the entrants in the early singlehanded races across the Atlantic chose Contessa 26s, and they were also well represented in the Round Britain and Ireland Race.

The English boat-building firm of Jeremy Rogers first began building the Contessa 26 in 1966, and the demand for them was so great that in the first three years of production alone, 350 of the fiberglass hulls were laid up. But molds were shipped in 1969 to Toronto, Canada, where the firm of J. J. Taylor & Sons also started production. In 1983, the Canadian firm redesigned the deck and interior, and started using lead ballast instead of iron, which lowered the cabin sole and gave more headroom. A year later, the Canadian manufacturer dropped the name Contessa 26 and changed it to the J. J. Taylor 26.

Some 400 Contessa/Taylor 26s were built in Canada, and many of them found their way to the United States where they are still going strong.

Basic Design

When you look at the lines of the Contessa 26 you can't help but think "Folkboat." The raking stern with its outboard rudder; the long, curved tiller; the sweeping sheerline; that gracious bow overhang: they're all signs of her Folkboat heritage. That's where her seaworthy genes came from, and her classic Scandinavian good looks. But perhaps it would be more accurate to describe her as a Folkboat modernized and improved.

She's thoroughly traditional, with her full-length keel, but her masthead sloop rig is taller and skinnier, her foresail bigger, more efficient, and more powerful to windward. A smidgen more beam has improved her accommodations without destroying her performance under sail, and a tip-tilt main hatchway has given her 5 feet 8 inches of headroom below – at least over a small portion of the cabin.

The hull is solid fiberglass, and the decks and cabintop are fiberglass cored with edge-grain balsa. Balsa is good for insulation, and it's pretty effective at containing water damage to a small area. Nevertheless, deck leaks over a long period can lead to delamination, so check all the upper surfaces of the boat carefully if you're buying an older model.

The cockpit is of average size for a boat of this displacement, and is self-draining, but might with advantage be made smaller for extended ocean passages. If a breaking wave fills it, the boat will become vulnerable to the next wave approaching from astern, because she does not have excessive freeboard.

Taylor models built after hull #300 incorporated an anchor well in the bow for the first time, which created handy stowage for the ground tackle and kept the foredeck clear of toe-stubbing obstructions.

The standard engine is the 7-hp Farymann, a single-cylinder, raw-water-cooled diesel thumper that is reputed to use only 1 quart of fuel an hour at a cruising speed touching 5 knots. As the Contessa's fuel tank holds 12 gallons, that indicates a range under power in calm conditions of 240 miles.

Maximum power is developed at 2,500 rpm, but the propeller shaft, working through a 2-to-1-reduction gearbox, runs at only half that speed, pushing a 12-inch diameter x 9-inch pitch two-bladed prop. It's a no-frills engine installation with a reputation for reliability, but it's neither smooth nor restful in action, and you continually need to make sure it can't succeed in its frenzied efforts to shake itself loose from the engine bearers.

In Short

**Contessa 26/
J.J. Taylor 26**

Designer: David Sadler
(1966)

LOA: 25 feet 6 inches

LWL: 21 feet 0 inches

Beam: 7 feet 6 inches

Draft: 4 feet 0 inches

Displacement: 5,400 pounds

Sail area: 280 square feet

Ballast: Encapsulated iron or lead

Spars: Aluminum

Auxiliary: Diesel, 7 hp.

Designed as: Seaworthy racer/cruiser

Accommodations

There is a small bulkheaded forepeak right up forward that acts as a chain locker. It's not the best place for much weight, so close to the bow, but there's not much choice. Aft of the chain locker comes the usual forecabin, dominated by a V-berth with stowage and tankage beneath it. If you're planning to sail a 26 around the world, you'd be better off with a workbench and more stowage space up there. You're not likely to want to cross an ocean with four people on board in a boat this small unless you're also interested in hair shirts and self-flagellation. Aft of the V-berth there's a hanging locker to

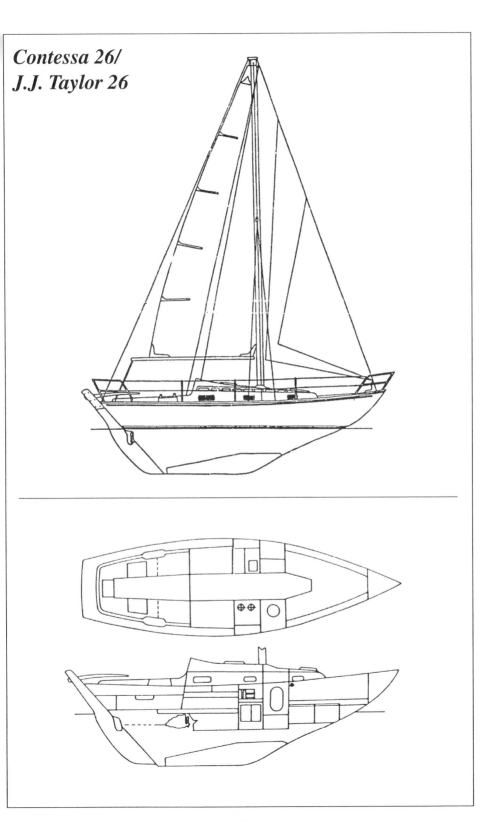

*Contessa 26/
J.J. Taylor 26*

port and a head compartment to starboard. Then comes a split galley, a good way to provide decent working space for the cook in a boat of this size, although some people find it easier to cook in the usual place under the main sliding hatch, where the light and ventilation are a lot better. On the Contessa, the stove and a top-opening icebox are to starboard, while the sink and counter space are to port.

Aft of the galley there are settee berths on either side, the ends of which tuck under the cockpit seats. Removable companionway steps on the centerline give access to the engine compartment, and you can also get to the engine through a panel in the cockpit sole, but it's mighty cramped in there. There are two large opening hatches on the later Taylor 26 models, one in the forecabin and another conveniently above the galley area. They help distribute light and air down below, but some people still find the living quarters of the 26 rather cave-like because there is no sliding hatch over the main companionway. Instead, the coachroof slopes up sharply at its after end to form what amounts to a half-round solid dodger, except that it doesn't extend aft over the cockpit. It looks like the back hoop of a prairie schooner. Some people call it a bubble, others call it a hump. Whatever it is, it's quirky. It makes the entrance to the cabin very strong and seaworthy, but it takes some getting used to.

The Rig

The rig is strong and simple – she's a single-spreader, masthead sloop with fore and aft lower shrouds. The forestay is housed well inboard so you can sit down, wedge yourself in the pulpit facing aft, and handle the staysail from up forward if you need to.

The sail area is modest – the mainsail has an area of just 154 square feet. She's designed to take a No. 1 genoa of 251 square feet, a No. 2 genoa of 208 square feet, and a No. 3 genoa of 178 square feet. The working jib has an area of 126 square feet, and the storm jib is a very manageable 70 square feet. The spars are anodized aluminum, the reefing is jiffy, and the mainsheet secures at the aft end of the cockpit. All very standard and well tested. No surprises here.

Performance

The Contessa 26's PHRF rating is 252, exactly the same as the Nordic Folkboat and the Cape Dory 25D. With her 21-foot waterline, her maximum sustained speed is a little over 6 knots, but of more importance for deepsea cruising is the fact that she'll reach a high percentage of her top speed fairly easily under sail, without being overpressed. That adds up to good daily runs and fast passages.

The design has proved docile and well mannered under all conditions. Tania Aebi proved that the Contessa 26 could be handled with perfect confidence by a 95-pound woman.

Known Weaknesses

• As on all boats with balsa-cored decks and coachroofs, watch out for hollow-sounding areas where water may have entered and begun the delamination process.

• Some owners have added a shoe to the aft end of the keel. It overlaps the bottom of the rudder, and prevents stray lines from jamming between the rudder and the keel.

• Depending on the boat's fore-and-aft trim, the scuppers on the side decks may not be able to drain all the water that gathers there. Some owners have made new scuppers in better places.

• If you're venturing into stormy waters, you may want to beef up the rudder with a third pintle and gudgeon, just in case.

Owner's Opinion

B. J. Calwell's *Mai (Miti) Vavau* was rolled over in the stormy Indian Ocean. One night, at midnight, with the trade winds blowing at 40 knots, he heard the deafening roar of a breaking wave approaching from astern. An explosion engulfed the boat, he said, and she was rolled upside down. He found himself lying on the cabin roof inside the main saloon and praying for his boat to right herself.

As the ballast keel slowly pulled her back upright, he pulled out a hatchboard and scanned the deck for damage. Miraculously, he said, the mast was still up and in one piece, but the rest of the boat was in complete disarray.

> ### In Comparison
> • Safety-at-sea factor: 11 (Rated against the 19 other boats in this book, with 1 being safest.)
> • Speed rating: PHRF 252. A good performer, particularly on long ocean passages.
> • Ocean comfort level: One or two adults in as much comfort as might be expected in a two-tonner, which is not much.

Although it took him the rest of the night to restore order, the only permanent damage he found was a blown-out staysail and a broken solar panel. He faced another severe test when he rounded Cape Agulhas, also known as the Cape of Storms. In fact, southwesterly gales blowing over the fast-flowing Agulhas Current forced him back into port five times over a period of two months, but his boat survived without serious damage.

Tania Aebi also experienced her share of heavy weather and frights, but *Varuna* also escaped permanent damage. Both skippers were of the opinion that they could not have found a stronger, more seaworthy boat for the price.

Conclusion

This is a Folkboat that has grown a little wider, a little longer, a little deeper, and a little heavier. She somehow doesn't look as delicately pretty as a Folkboat, but she's probably more seaworthy, if that's possible. Her trademark companionway hump makes for accommodation that resembles a badly lit, cramped dentist's waiting room – unless a large opening hatch has been fitted overhead – but it does provide reassuringly solid shelter and separation from bad weather.

If you're serious about cruising, and especially if you're a singlehander, this boat will perform well and look after you when the chips are down. She's small enough to give you the feeling that you're always in control, but large and tough enough to survive really bad weather. For somewhere around $15,000, you should be able to find one in reasonable condition. Good seaboats don't come much cheaper than that.

Chapter Ten
Contessa 32

She's a Many-Talented Aristocrat

A Contessa 32 named *Assent* was fated to go down in nautical history when she was the only yacht in her class to finish a race marred by a storm so bad that five boats sank, 19 were abandoned, and 15 competitors were drowned. It was the infamous Fastnet Race of 1979, in which 303 yachts were overwhelmed by 65-knot winds between England and Ireland.

Assent's success assured her, and her British designer, David Sadler, of instant fame. Sales of the already-popular racer/cruiser soared, and the boat became the subject of intense scrutiny by safety committees and experts interested in finding out what made her so seaworthy. The fascinating fact was that the Contessa 32 was a fin-keeler, with a detached rudder set on a skeg, not the kind of full-keeled design traditionally associated with good seakeeping.

She turned out to be a very moderate boat, a clever transition between the traditional heavy-displacement Bristol Channel cutters, or Falmouth Quay punts, and the modern lightweights designed to the IOR rule, with lots of beam and high centers of gravity.

Sadler created a boat with a displacement-to-length ratio of 310, which placed her firmly in the medium-displacement class. Her beam was quite narrow – 9 feet 6 inches on a 24-foot waterline – and her center of gravity was kept low by a draft of 5 feet 6 inches and a ballast keel weighing 4,500 pounds. That's a whopping 47 percent of her total designed displacement. So the Contessa 32 ended up with a very wide range of positive stability, plus the promise of a quick recovery in the event of a 180-degree capsize. And, as competitors in that ill-fated Fastnet Race discovered, even the most seaworthy of yachts can be turned upside down by a plunging breaker that is big enough. Under survival conditions, ultimate stability, or the speed with which a boat will pull herself upright after a capsize, becomes of more importance than initial stability, which storm waves can and do overcome.

It was difficult in those days for the traditionalists to accept that a fin-and-skeg boat could be as seaworthy as a full-keeled Colin Archer or a pilot cutter. In fact, to this day there are people who won't have it. But what *Assent* proved in practice, Tony Marchaj and other marine researchers proved in theory, namely, that there is nothing inherently unseaworthy about a correctly-designed fin-keeler.

The difference between a Contessa 32 and most other fin keelers, of course, is that she is deep and narrow, as opposed to shallow and wide. Shallow-and-wide usually translates into more speed than deep-and-narrow. It also provides more room down below. It's lighter, and cheaper. So, naturally, it's more popular with the builders and the public. Most people, after all, are happy to trade a bit of seaworthiness in return for more speed and accommodation. Only those who want to cross oceans, or sail in all conditions with an easy mind, will appreciate the extra seaworthiness the slower, more cramped Contessa 32 provides.

Basic Design

This boat was touched by magic from the start. When she was introduced to the public at the International Boat Show in London in 1973, she walked away with the coveted Boat of the Show Award. Her builders, the Jeremy Rogers Boatyard, in Lymington, prepared for the rush, and between then and 1982 they turned out more than 700 boats.

At the same time, however, the Contessa 32 was being built under license in Canada by the J. J. Taylor company in Ontario. Their production run ended in 1990, by which time 87 Contessa 32s had been built. Many of them have since found their way to the United States.

She was designed to do well in offshore races organized by the British Royal Ocean Racing Club (RORC), and while her fin-and-skeg underbody made her reasonably fast, it was her reputation for seaworthiness that really got the attention of long-distance cruisers. It has been calculated that she will heel over to 157 degrees from the vertical before she loses the ability to right herself.

Besides finishing the 1979 Fastnet Race, Contessa 32s have been used for a singlehanded circumnavigation and a double-handed rounding of Cape Horn the "wrong way" – against the prevailing storm winds.

Although she is technically a fin-keeler, the Contessa 32's fin is quite large in area by today's standards, and extends a long way fore and aft. It's as if one of Ted Brewer's trademark "bites" had been taken out of the aft end of a full keel, leaving a truncated long keel and a stubby little skeg. The skeg runs the full length of the rudder, making it a very strong installation, and the rounded, cut-away forefoot of the keel makes her reasonably easy to manage downwind. The bottom of the keel is flat for several feet, so she can dry out against a harbor wall or post without too much fuss.

She appears to have a straight sheerline but in fact there is just enough spring to the sheer to prevent her from looking humpbacked, and the lowest part of the gunwale lies slightly forward of the cockpit.

The Contessa's cockpit is quite long and comfortable. High coamings provide excellent shelter at the helm, and a strong bridgedeck separates the cockpit well from the main saloon. Access to the clear foredeck is reasonably easy, thanks to wide sidedecks.

A tiller was the standard fitting, but a wheel was offered as an option, and most owners seem to have taken

---

In Short

Contessa 32

Designer: David Sadler (1972)

LOA: 32 feet 0 inches

LWL: 24 feet 0 inches

Beam: 9 feet 6 inches

Draft: 5 feet 6 inches

Displacement: 9,500 pounds

Sail area: 562 square feet

Ballast: 4,500 pounds, lead

Spars: Aluminum

Auxiliary: Diesel, 12 to 28 hp.

Designed as: Ocean racer/ fast cruiser

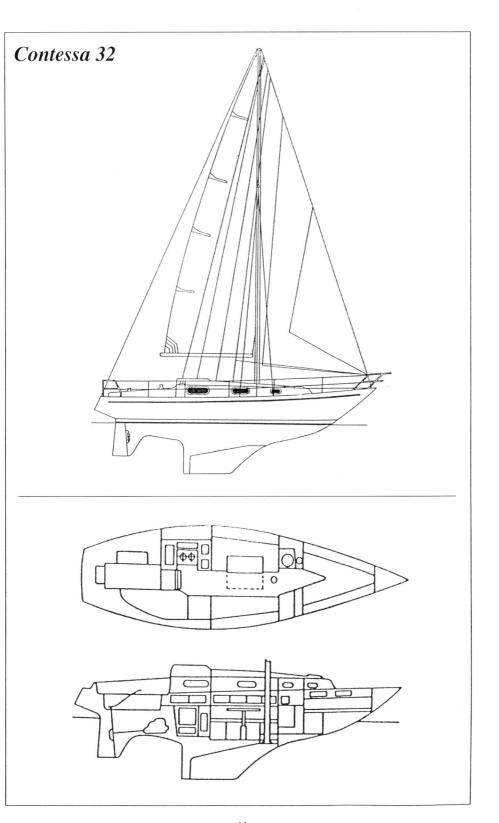

Contessa 32

the option, not because steering with a tiller was difficult but because a wheel frees up more cockpit space.

Accommodations

You'll notice the difference between a British-built Contessa 32 and a Canadian-built one in the accommodations. Both used the same basic layout, but while British boats were finished completely in wood down below, the Canadian manufacturer used white fiberglass moldings trimmed with wood. The interior is cramped by modern standards, although trading interior space for seaworthiness is not a bad plan in a long-distance cruiser. In any case, this is a boat for one or two people, no more – except, of course, for weekend sailing. Headroom varies from 6 feet 1 inch to about 5 feet 10 inches. There's a chain locker and V-berth up forward, followed by a head to port and a hanging locker to starboard. The main saloon has a narrow double-berth to port and a single to starboard. The U-shaped galley lies to port, and opposite there is the luxury of a dedicated chart table, although the navigator must sit on the head of anyone sleeping in the quarterberth tucked in behind it. Incidentally, that makes six berths in all– four too many for long-distance cruising if you wish to retain your sanity.

Most Contessa 32s were fitted with diesel engines of decent size, starting with the 24-hp Farymann, and changing over at intervals to the 20-hp Bukh, the 28-hp Volvo, and the 27-hp Yanmar. Owners of Contessas with engines of 12 hp or less complain about lack of reserve power.

The Rig

She has a single-spreader masthead sloop rig that could be converted to a cutter for cruising or rule-cheating purposes, but is otherwise unremarkable. Her mainsail has a high aspect ratio, efficiently tall and thin, and her foresail area is large, so you'll need powerful, easily managed sheet winches in the cockpit.

It's obviously a strong rig. Several Contessas sailing in marginal conditions have dipped their masts under water and survived with the rig standing, but you'd want to replace the whole gang of rigging as a matter of principle before leaving on an ocean voyage.

The main boom is short, barely overlapping the forward end of the cockpit, which results in an awkward sheeting position just aft of the companionway entrance. On a cruising boat, a longer, heftier boom might enable the mainsheet track to be set up well aft, clear of the helm and crew.

Performance

Good all-round performance is the hallmark of this Sadler design but, as already noted, she gets an A+ for heavy-weather work. Declan Mackell, who sailed *Sean-Ois* around the world singlehanded between 1979 and 1983, reported a day's run of 186 miles between the Canaries and Barbados. She really shouldn't have done better than 157 miles, because her theoretical maximum hull speed is 6.56 knots, but sometimes there's a little magic that helps the Irish do better than other mortals. In any case, this boat is no mean performer under twin running sails in the trades.

Known Weaknesses

• You'll need to figure out how to carry more fresh water, since the water tank encapsulated in the keel holds only 15 imperial gallons.

• The double berth to port is really a wide single. Don't get any fancy ideas.

• Check the chainplates. There have been reports of failures.

Owner's Opinion

British physicist Alex Nichol owned a Contessa 32 called *Royal Crescent* with a partner for 18 years, sailing her out of Parkstone Yacht Club in Poole, Dorset. His cruising grounds encompassed the English Channel and the French coast from Cherbourg to the mouth of the Loire – an area known for sudden storms and short choppy seas.

"It's a very strong and seaworthy basic design," he says, "but for long-distance heavy work some reinforcement of the bow is required. We had a pair of extra foam stringers molded in from the head compartment forward."

He advises buyers of used boats to check the shroud plates, and possibly to strengthen them. "The other point of weakness is the forestay tack fitting – this is a 3/8-inch stainless steel U-bolt, and ours just broke one day in quite moderate weather. It was what the metallurgists call a 'corrosion crack' where a tiny superficial crack at deck level corroded in and then failed. We had a new fitting made to wrap over the stemhead and bolted it through."

Royal Crescent's mast developed corrosion under the fittings just above deck level after about 12 years and was replaced as a precaution.

Nichol detected no sign of osmosis in the hull, even when the boat was approaching 20 years of age. "The rudder is on a very heavy skeg and should give no worries. We had some work done at 16 years, but that kind of thing is to be expected. A point to note, however, is that if you *do* have to do anything to the rudder or engine shaft, you have to start by cutting off the bottom tip of the skeg, where it wraps around below the bottom of the rudder, so as to get that the deeply embedded lower pintle."

Royal Crescent points well, tacking through just under 70 degrees with the original Hood #1 genoa. She starts to get weather helm at about 15 knots of windspeed, Nichol notes, but it's easily cured by reefing. "You should reef the mainsail first. Then she will re-balance and go faster. A second reef in the mainsail, with a suitable foresail, makes her easy to handle in any wind up to Force 7." He once beat 70 miles across the Channel in a Force 7 wind. That's 28 to 33 knots, and officially described as a "near-gale."

"We got caught in Alderney, in the Channel Islands, by a northeasterly blow that came up from nothing, and had to get back to Poole. We hoisted a double-reefed main and a small jib. She just loved it, and we were sailing past other boats of similar size which were wallowing – probably because they were over canvassed."

In Comparison

• Safety-at-sea factor: 2 (Rated against the 19 other boats in this book, with 1 being safest.)

• Speed rating: PHRF rating 189. Fast for a cruiser, but slower than modern race boats.

• Ocean comfort level: One or two adults in comfort; two adults and two kids in less comfort. In racing trim (no comfort) she sleeps five.

Nichol feels it pays to reef the Contessa early. "Indeed, our boat would sail to windward very happily on just a foresail – a flat-cut, rather heavy #2 genoa designed for roller reefing." The Contessa's performance under headsail alone is exceptional.

"One day we were going from Treguier to Lesardrieux through the Passe de la Gaine and Moisie channels. It was a dead run down the Gaine, so rather than have the mainsail blanket the foresail, and have the mainsail jibe back and forth, we put up just the #2 genoa. It was then a nice reach into the Moisie under just that sail, so we left it. We came around into the Grand Chenal to Lesardrieux and I said: 'Let's see if she'll lay it.' And she did – overhauling a lot of French boats that were beating and wondering how on earth we were doing it."

According to Nichol, the Contessa's galley is adequate for extended cooking while living on board, and well placed for use at sea.

He also feels the cockpit is about the right size for ocean work, although it gets rather wet during a beat to windward in a blow. "By modern standards, the Contessas are low in freeboard." *Royal Crescent* had a Yanmar, single-cylinder 12-hp diesel engine, which Nichol found a little lacking in power. "I would prefer a little more power in reserve, and two cylinders. The 18-hp Bukh is reckoned to be the best of the various ones installed as standard. The Yanmar's great merit was an incredibly low fuel consumption– about 4 or 5 hours to the British gallon."

Finally, one of Nichol's favorite cruising anecdotes:

"We were sailing in the Morbihan (northwest France) between the two major islands, where the direction of buoyage is not obvious. We knew where we were, and had a large-scale chart. Halfway, near a channel buoy, we came upon a large French yacht on the wrong side of it, hard aground – and apparently trying to haul himself even further aground with a kedge.

"As we came up, he made great gesticulations, pointing at the buoy and waving us to pass well on his side of it. As we complacently slid by on the other side, realization hit him. A great cry of 'Merde!' came across the water."

Chapter Eleven
Dana 24

This Seductress Has Hidden Charms

The Dana 24 has always reminded me of Cinderella. Down below, she's Cinderella at the ball before midnight – glittering and glamorous. On deck, she's Cinderella at home – quite plain and not looking her best.

If you can get past this little boat's lumpy looks, you'll discover she has a heart of gold. If you can't – well, shame on you. And be careful what you say about her. Forget that she's more dumpy than dainty. There are many handsome princes out there who are smitten with her charms, and who will defend her honor at all costs.

This is the second smallest boat in the series of production boats manufactured by the Pacific Seacraft Corporation (PS) in California. PS has earned a nation-wide reputation for quality boatbuilding, and the Dana 24 is a tough, rugged ocean cruiser built to very high specifications. There's nothing you have to do structurally to a Dana to make her fit for sea. She comes that way. She's an out-and-out cruiser, designed for safety and comfort without any concern for racing rules, though that doesn't necessarily make her slow, as her designer, William Crealock, will tell you.

Crealock is thorough and cautious, a conservative member of the old school who was trained the proper way. He began his career in Scotland, where one of his first jobs was to design a ship's bulkhead. It took him a week.

The Dana is the synthesis of Crealock's knowledge of, and respect for, the sea and PS's commitment to the best materials and building methods. And she has proved a winner.

She has also proved expensive. A brand new one, hot off the press, will cost you $99,400 before tax, and you'll probably have to spend a few thousand more on the odds and ends needed for an ocean voyage. No small amount for a 24-footer. But for quite a lot of people the price just doesn't matter. After all, if you're madly in love with Cinderella, what option do you have?

Basic Design

The Dana 24 is 24 feet on deck, 27 feet overall and 21 feet on the waterline. Her nose is snub and nearly plumb, and her topsides are high for her length. Her stern is a stubby, no-nonsense transom, and under water she carries a full-length keel vigorously cut away up forward for almost half the length of the boat. And sitting on top of everything there is that lofty, box of a cabin with ports that stare at you like the oversized eyes of an African bush baby startled by the beam of a flashlight.

Her squared-off rudder pivots from the end of the keel, which ends a little way forward of the transom, and the after end of the rudder projects past the transom under water. The cutout for the propeller is taken entirely from the deadwood of the keel, so she is assured of efficient steering.

A glance at her decks is all that's needed to tell you what this boat is designed for. She has a true bluewater cruiser's bulwarks edging her decks all around, a full 5 inches deep in places. Her bowsprit is short, less than 3 feet, in fact, but it helps make a cutter of her and gives her a salty air of jauntiness. It has a bronze eyeband, and in fact everywhere you look on deck you'll find fittings of solid bronze, including winches, cleats, and chocks.

To the untrained eye, the cockpit looks small, but the seats are long enough to lie down on – 6 feet 3 inches, to be precise. The seat backs are contoured for comfort, and high coamings provide a welcome feeling of security as well as protection from bad weather. With a solid bridgedeck and two 1 1/2-inch drains for fast self-bailing, this is a proper seagoing cockpit. A 10-pound propane tank lives in a cockpit storage locker with its own hatch, and a manual bilge pump is mounted through the cockpit seat riser so you can reach it from the helm.

As a final touch, PS has built a watertight access hatch into the cockpit sole so you can easily get to those parts of the engine that need regular attention. The power plant is the twin-cylinder Yanmar 2GM20F, which develops 18 horsepower – enough to keep the Dana 24 charging along at hull speed of a little over 6 knots in almost any conditions.

Accommodations

When you step down below on a Dana 24 you step into another world. She's palatial for a boat only 21 feet on the waterline. Her open-plan design melds the forepeak and the main saloon into one cabin whose length, breadth, and depth make you wonder if you've lost all sense of proportion.

The vinyl cabin headliner is 6 feet above the teak-and-holly sole for a start – now you know why the coachroof sticks up so much – and the forward V-berth is 6 feet 8 inches long and 6 feet 9 inches wide. That headliner, incidentally, is fastened in place by zippers, so you can easily remove it to get at electrical wiring and the inside end of fastenings for deck fittings.

Most of the interior is a fiberglass molding firmly bonded to the hull, but it's smothered in bright, hand-rubbed, oiled teak so well crafted that it wouldn't be out of place in a Victorian gentleman's club if it were darker and more tobacco-stained. Everywhere you look, you get the feeling that opulence is held in check only by practical seamanship. The gleaming portlight surrounds, the meticulously finished cabinet work, the cleverly contrived sliding/hiding table – everything down below gives the impression that it is not only highly pedigreed, but also on its best behavior. This is, of course, no less than would expect to find in a $100,000 boat, but it comes as more of a surprise on such a small one.

In Comparison

- Safety-at-sea factor: 16 (Rated against the 19 other boats in this book, with 1 being safest.)
- Speed rating: She's not fast, especially when loaded for cruising, but she's capable of making good time on long passages off the wind.
- Ocean comfort level: One or two adults in comfort.

Dana 24

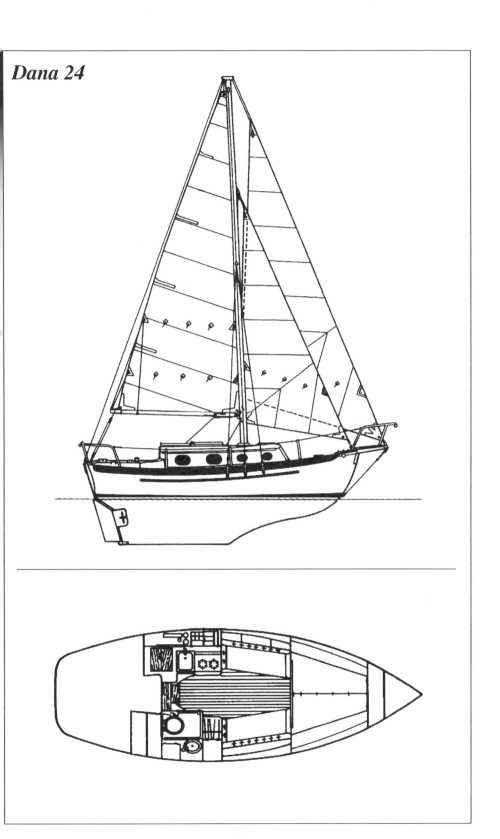

There is no bulkhead between the large V-berth up forward and the main cabin, which boasts two 6-foot 6-inch settee berths. Aft of the settees there is a full-sized, enclosed head to starboard and a surprisingly large galley to port, complete with a 4.5 cubic-foot icebox, a stainless steel sink, and a four-burner propane stove with oven. Overhead, two teak grabrails run the length of the cabin. You'll bless them at sea. The standard water tank holds 40 gallons, a lot for this size of boat, but you can also have an additional 30-gallon tank built in at additional cost. The fuel tank holds 18 gallons of diesel, and the head holding tank has a capacity of 15 gallons.

The Rig

Pacific Seacraft offers all of its sailboats as cutters or sloops, and although you might regard the Dana 24 as being a little small for a cutter rig, it does divide the sail area into small units for easier handling. The sail area of the sloop is nominally 358 square feet, while the cutter's area is 448 square feet. The mainsail on this efficient, high-aspect-ratio rig has an area of just over 140 square feet. The sloop rig will be the better performer to windward, with its single headsail, and only one stay and one set of running rigging to create windage, but the cutter might be more convenient if you're short-handed. It also has the advantage that you can mount the jib on a roller furler and simply make it disappear when the wind pipes up, without ever being forced to reef it. That leaves the sturdy little staysail to do the heavy work and means you'll never be shamed in public by a baggy, badly setting, inefficient, 150-percent genoa reefed down to the size of a storm jib. Both rigs run to the masthead, and the inner forestay of the cutter, running almost parallel to the jibstay, terminates at the stemhead. Incidentally, the standard hank-on jib supplied with the boat has a built-in row of reef points – something you won't find on your namby-pamby, common-or-garden coastal cruiser. The aluminum mast is stepped on deck in a stainless steel tabernacle, and because there is no bulkhead in the cabin below it, a sturdy stainless steel compression post delivers the downward thrust straight to the keel. The mast and boom are painted with a linear polyurethane finish.

It's a bit of a stretch aft from the end of the boom to the mainsheet track on the afterdeck, which results in some slight inefficiency of angle and extra torture for the boom on the beat, but it's a worthwhile compromise to keep the sheet clear of the cockpit.

All in all, it's a simple, sturdy rig eminently fit for sea work.

Performance

William Crealock is a designer who knows how to coax good performance out of cruising boats, and by cruising boats we mean small boats with a lot of accommodations and the ability to carry a heavy load of water and stores.

His designs might not be the nippiest around the buoys in a Saturday afternoon club race because they do not have the swift acceleration of a lightweight racer, but he has learned to refine the underwater lines so that his boats are able to reach their maximum hull speeds with the minimum of fuss and power. This means they are easily driven, and quickly reach and maintain respectable cruising speeds. It's what all cruising boat designers strive for, of course, but not all find the magic formula.

The Dana 24 is a heavy displacement boat, but heavy displacement is no barrier to good performance if the rig that drives is its powerful enough and efficient enough. On the Dana it is both.

Her long keel gives her excellent directional stability, and that cutaway forefoot might have been deliberately designed with those rolling trade wind swells in mind. She'll romp down their faces as if she were on tracks. But her moderate draft also enables her to gunkhole and explore the thin waters of the world – the fascinating reefs and shallows– that are so often the best reward for crossing an ocean.

Known Weaknesses

She is a shameless seductress. Beware. You could find yourself falling in love with this boat without warning and running away to foreign places with her.

Owner's Opinion

Bill and Lola Hotard sail their Dana 24, *Lola*, out of Mariner's Cove, on Whidbey Island, Washington. Last summer they headed north to Alaska, cruising 1,700 miles in 11 weeks to Wrangel and back with their dog Magruder, a cross cocker spaniel/poodle. Bill has a deep knowledge of sailboat cruising and believes in conservative sailing.

Lola is rigged as a sloop at the moment, with a 130-percent genoa on a roller furler. But Bill wants to change that.

"When we're going to windward I start reefing the genoa first, at about 10 or 12 knots. But the reefed genoa doesn't perform well in heavy winds. The shape is wrong, and she won't point." So Bill is planning to instal a staysail and change *Lola* to a cutter.

"She starts to get weather helm as the wind comes up," he said, "but it's curable by reefing. With the cutter rig, I'll take the first reef in the mainsail at about 12 knots. Then, if the wind is still rising, I'll furl the genoa completely, leaving just the staysail forward of the mast. At about 18 to 20 knots I'll take in the second reef in the mainsail."

Bill has had a third set of reef points built into the main to reduce its area to about 60 square feet. The staysail, with an area of 90 square feet, also can be reefed down to 60 square feet.

Under motor, *Lola* gets 5 1/2 knots from her Yanmar 2GM20 18-hp diesel engine at about 75 percent power. "She runs for about 3 hours on a gallon of fuel at that speed," Bill said, "but if you reduce speed to 5 knots or a bit less she'll give you 21 miles to the gallon in calm water."

The Hotards found the Dana 24's accommodation comfortable for two and a dog. "I'm 6 feet 5 inches tall, so I have to bend my head a bit unless I'm under the hatch," Bill said, "but to tell the truth I don't find myself standing up much when I'm down below anyway." Lola, a gourmet cook, had plenty of headroom in the galley.

In Short

Dana 24

Designer: William Crealock

LOA: 27 feet 3 inches

LOD: 24 feet 2 inches

LWL: 21 feet 5 inches

Beam: 8 feet 7 inches

Draft: 3 feet 10 inches

Displacement: 8,000 pounds

Sail area: 358 square feet

Ballast: Lead, 3,200 pounds

Spars: Aluminum

Auxiliary: Yanmar diesel 18 hp

Designed as: A salty, roomy heavy-displacement cruiser

Bill felt the size of the cockpit might with benefit be reduced for an ocean crossing, in case it got filled with water. "I'd keep the rolled-up inflatable dinghy in the cockpit to reduce its capacity," he said, "and perhaps a couple of fuel or water jugs as well."

He'd augment the boat's 40-gallon fresh water supply with a 12-volt watermaker that could also be operated manually if necessary, and he'd probably tuck away a couple of 5-gallon collapsible plastic jugs of drinking water as insurance. He is a staunch advocate of jacklines, safety harnesses, and tethers. He runs flat nylon straps from padeyes up forward back to the cockpit, and hooks his tether on to them when he's moving about on deck. He has two tethers on his harness, one of 6 feet and one of 3 feet, for close-up work. Inside the cockpit he has run lines fore and aft on either side, to which he clips his short tether in bad weather.

"Another item you'd need for offshore work would be a wind vane self-steering gear," he said. "I'd probably choose a Monitor because it doesn't have dissimilar metals to cause electrolytic corrosion problems.

Finally, he recommended that light-weather sails be given serious consideration for an ocean crossing. "She's slow in light weather under her working sails. I'd definitely want an asymmetrical spinnaker and maybe a nylon ghoster for close reaching."

Conclusion

Let's face it, there are cheaper ways to cross an ocean. The Dana 24 represents a considerable financial outlay. On the other hand, she comes complete with an extraordinary amount of equipment of the highest quality. You could compare her, perhaps, to the smaller models of the Mercedes-Benz automobile, the Mercedes being the Dana 24 of cars. After all, what other 24-footers deliver such standard features as a ballbearing mainsheet traveler, two bow anchor rollers, a swim ladder with teak treads, and a stern chain locker (with roller and deck pipe) to match the one in the bow?

Chapter Twelve
Falmouth Cutter 22

Here's a Small but Precious Package

The coastline is rugged and convoluted around Falmouth, Cornwall. The tides run fast and the wind blows stormily from the southwest. A boat under sail needs to be strong, buoyant, agile, and weatherly to survive those conditions. Just like the Falmouth Cutter 22, in fact.

At first glance, you wouldn't connect Lyle Hess's feisty little cutter with that coastline. She looks too small, too vulnerable– and perhaps too darned cocky for her own good. But, in fact, in every respect except size, she shares the properties that earned the renowned Falmouth cutters their reputation for safety and seaworthiness.

She's old-fashioned, deliberately old-fashioned, as if she's delighting in carrying on an ancient tradition of full keels and simple fittings in an era when fin keels and electronic gimmicks rule the roost.

Hess designed this cutter with no regard for racing rules or modern fads. His aim was to create a pocket cruiser that could cross oceans, and his foremost concern was safety. You'll notice her resemblance to her bigger sister the 28-foot Bristol Channel Cutter. In fact, only minor changes were dictated by her smaller size.

Although it wasn't a design priority, the Falmouth 22, with her 8-foot beam, turned out to be trailerable. She is not the sort of trailer sailer you tow behind the family car and launch into the nearest lake for a Saturday afternoon jaunt, however. In the first place, she weighs 7,400 pounds, and you'll need at least a Suburban or a full-size pickup with which to tow her. In the second place, it would take you most of the afternoon to get her mast and rigging set up properly.

But the fact that she's both trailerable and fully capable of ocean passages makes her very unusual, and very attractive to gentleman sailors who prefer not to sail to windward. For example, it's a nice downhill passage from Seattle to the Sea of Cortez, but it's a dreadful, endless slog against wind and current on the way back. But with a Falmouth cutter you can sail down in comfort and then tow her home against the prevailing wind at 50 miles an hour up Interstate 5.

Her shallow draft of 3 feet 6 inches gives her some wonderful advantages, too. She can sneak into pretty little coves and anchorages in the Florida Keys, or the Bahamas, that are denied to other ocean-going yachts with deep keels. And there's another thing about a small boat that is often overlooked. Many people actually feel safer and more confident on a smaller boat because they feel more in control at all times.

The sails are small and less of a handful to manage. The engine is small. You can probably start it by hand. The tiller never becomes unwieldy. You can paint the bottom in a couple of hours with a gallon of antifouling. Everything is more human-sized and manageable. And you never have to worry about your refrigeration going wrong, because you don't have room for a freezer in the first place.

Basic Design

The Falmouth Cutter 22 looks as if she should be built from wood. She has all those things that wooden boats have: bulwarks, a bowsprit, a boomkin, a tiller, a saucy sheerline, an outboard rudder, and a full keel. But she's made of fiberglass all right, and it's a solid, hand lay-up, not cored, so that the finished hull weighs about 1,100 pounds.

The Sam L. Morse Company, which builds the cutter in Costa Mesa, California, says the thickness of the hull varies from 5/16 inch at the sheer to 15/16 inch near the bottom of the hull. According to the company's sale brochure, "The actual thickness at the bottom of the keel is greater than 1 inch because we overlap layers at this location."

The lead ballast, a 2,500-pound block, is pre-cast and then placed inside the hull cavity. It's fixed in place by poured resin and covered with three layers of glass mat and roving. Unlike the hull, the 22's fiberglass deck does have a core. It's not the usual edge-grain balsa, however, but 1/2-inch marine plywood encapsulated in glass mat and 24-ounce roving. This makes a very strong, stiff deck on which you can mount hardware of your own without worrying about compressing the deck when you tighten the fasteners. Extra layers of plywood are used where the mast and mooring bitts penetrate the deck.

The sidedecks are reasonably wide and unobstructed by shrouds, which are taken outboard to their fullest extent for more efficient mast support, and you can do your work at the base of the mast in greater security because of the flat deck space between the coachroof and that cute little scuttle hatch a couple of feet forward of it.

Like her big sister, the Falmouth Cutter 22 has a plumb bow that sweeps around fairly sharply beneath the waterline and then takes an almost straight line aft to the deepest part of the keel under the cockpit. This is not exactly a high-lift airfoil fin, but it's alleged to be more efficient than it looks. Although it's long and shallow, Hess seems to have found a way to make this keel perform to windward. The sales brochure claims it gives the boat "as much or more windward ability and speed as other, now more common, cruising keels with skeg or spade rudders." In the absence of proof to the contrary, and making due allowance for the breathless prose of the sales staff, we must give the brochure the benefit of the doubt.

Her outboard rudder is attached directly to the keel and the transom, which lines up with the end of the keel. This is undoubtedly the simplest and strongest way to attach a rudder, and if anything should ever go wrong, it's the most accessible for repair.

The self-draining cockpit is small and shippy, safe at sea when you have to leave the boat to look after herself. The tiller sweeps over a good deal of it, but no bluewater sailor is going to complain about that. And in port you can remove the tiller and lock it down below for security reasons. Nothing deters a boat thief more than not being able to steer what he's stolen.

Most people will want the inboard engine with this boat, but depending on the kind of sailing you do most, it might also make a lot of sense to choose the outboard option. The inboard engine sits quite deep in the cutter's capacious nether regions; so

Falmouth Cutter 22

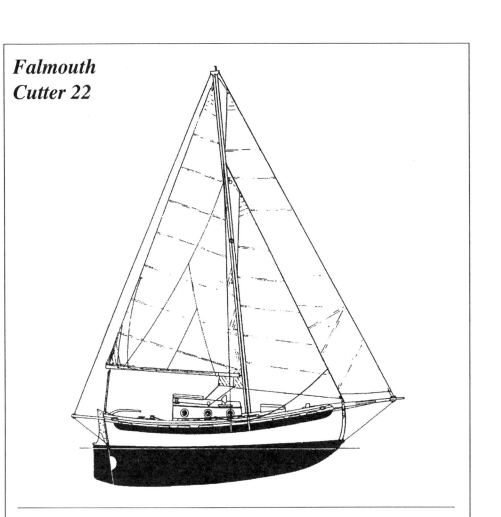

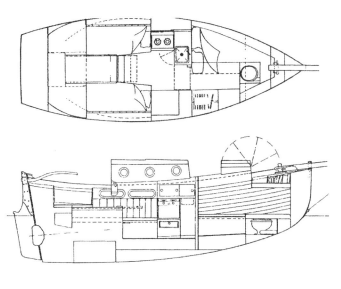

much so that the propeller shaft runs almost horizontally. The standard power plant is the Yanmar 1GM10, a single-cylinder, 9-hp diesel that drives a two-bladed, 14-inch by 10-inch prop. The 15-gallon fuel tank is situated under the cockpit, high enough in comparison with the engine to obviate any fuel lift problems. With this amount of fuel, and using about half a gallon an hour at full power, she'll have a range under power of about 180 miles at a little over 6 knots. Throttled back to a gentle cruise, she should do 250 miles or so at 4 1/2 to 5 knots in calm weather.

Accommodations

One of the first things you notice about the Falmouth Cutter 22 is that she's all wood down below. The Morse company does not use plastic hull liners or molds for the furniture. It's all done by hand from scratch. One big advantage here is that if you have any special requirements for the interior that differ from the standard layout, the company can build it exactly the way you want it and it may not even cost you any extra.

Practically speaking, the lack of liners means you can get to any part of the hull in a hurry, so if you have to stuff a blanket in a hole in the chine, you won't have to waste precious time chopping away acres of plastic.

There's headroom down below for all normal-sized people, at least under the cabin top and for a square foot or two under the hatch in the fo'c's'le, although you'll have to duck as you pass from one area to the other.

That forward cabin contains the head, a hanging locker, a vanity, and double berth to port. Alternatively, according to Roger Olson of the Sam L. Morse Co., you can have a double berth aft that runs athwartships, or even – if you opt for an outboard engine instead of an inboard – an enormous wall-to-wall passion pit. Some owners do opt for the outboard version, not necessarily for the voluptuous pleasures of the oversized bed, but, more prosaically, because of the large amount of stowage space it opens up.

Aft of the forward cabin, the galley lies to port, consisting of a large stainless steel sink, and a gimbaled twin-burner cooker with oven, with stowage outboard for dishes, cutlery, and condiments. Propane for the cooker is stored in aluminum tanks concealed in two mahogany deck boxes on either side of the mast. Across the gangway, to starboard, there's a big icebox with a top cover that doubles as a chart table.

Aft of the cooking/navigation area there are two settees that tuck in under the cockpit seats to become quarterberths. A table slides out from beneath the cockpit for use in the seating area.

The Rig

As her name implies, she has a simple, single-spreader, masthead rig of Bermudian mainsail and two headsails, a forestaysail, and a jib.

The 107-square-foot Yankee jib is flown from a bowsprit with just the right amount of steeve to create the illusion of a much larger boat, and the 98-square-foot staysail tacks down to the stemhead. The mainsail (171 square feet) is narrower and taller than you might expect on this type of boat, but its increased efficiency obviously contributes to good windward ability. The boom runs the full length from the mast to the transom, which makes for easy positioning of the mainsheet but tends to complicate the backstay arrangement. As a consequence, the backstay is led clear of the boom and the mainsail leech by a bumpkin that you could almost describe as petite if it weren't so determinedly rugged.

Performance

When we talk of performance we really mean two things: speed, especially to windward, and seakindliness. You have to be realistic about the speed of any boat that is less than 21 feet on the waterline and displaces more than 7,400 pounds. And then, having reined in your expectations, you can prepare to be pleasantly surprised. The Falmouth Cutter 22 is not going to sizzle around an Olympic course as would a club racer like a J-22 or even a Santana 22, but she will not disgrace herself in the company of other cruisers.

And when it comes to seakindliness and seaworthiness, she wins hands-down against the racers. She will keep going to weather in seas rough enough to knock the lightweight club racers back to the shelter of the yacht club bar. And in the trade winds she'll have that slow easy motion that makes a heavy displacement vessel so popular for long voyages, and she'll display her the ability to track down the face of large swells without the need for constant sawing at the helm and the constant wearying threat of broaching to.

Known Weaknesses

There must be some, apart from the "nuisance" weaknesses such as the bowsprit and bumpkin, but they are nowhere particularly evident.

The cockpit might be a little exposed in rough weather, perhaps, but we can hardly hold that against her. And by the time things are shaping up for a storm, you might want to shut yourself down below and let her look after herself.

Given that a good big boat is safer than a good small boat, the Falmouth Cutter 22's size is theoretically a weakness. She is so conservatively designed, however, and so ruggedly built, that you eventually are forced to the paradoxical conclusion that she suffers only from the best and strongest kind of weakness.

Owners' Opinions

People who own Falmouth Cutters are unreliable arbiters of her desirability. The kind of sailor who buys this boat is biased from the start, a hopeless romantic who knows from the beginning that only a boat with charm, character, craggy good looks, and the highest standards of seakindliness will satisfy him. Or her, as it happens. Several women have crossed oceans in them.

Mary White, owner of Sapo, sailed singlehanded. After the 31-day crossing from Mexico to the Marquesas, she said she gave thanks to Lyle Hess and the Sam. L. Morse company every day. And when she got farther west she added: "People keep asking to buy my boat, I even

---

In Short
Falmouth Cutter 22
Designer: Lyle Hess
LOA: 30 feet 6 inches
LOD: 22 feet 0 inches
LWL: 20 feet 10 inches
Beam: 8 feet 0 inches
Draft: 3 feet 6 inches
Displacement: 7,400 pounds
Sail area: 403 square feet
Ballast: Lead, 2,500 pounds
Spars: Aluminum
Auxiliary: Yanmar 1GM10 9-hp diesel
Designed as: Trailerable pocket ocean cruiser

have an offer here in Tonga."

Some restless people truck their Falmouth Cutters all over the place. Gary Felton sailed his boat, *Angelsea*, direct from San Diego to Cabo San Lucas, Mexico. After 7 months in the Sea of Cortez, he borrowed a trailer and took her back to San Diego. Then he trucked her to Fort Lauderdale, Florida, and made a 21-day trip to the Virgin Islands.

Mitch Kilgore ran into heavy weather with his *Hopscotch* en route to the Bahamas. "As soon as it got dark the wind freshened to 25 knots and the seas built to 8 to 10 feet." The cutter kept beating hard to windward with plenty of spray and great motion, yet Kilgore felt quite safe. "*Hopscotch* was in her element," he said. "The crossing was somewhat scary for my family, but they got over it fast, being preoccupied with the Bahamas. I bet if more gentlemen owned Sam L. Morse boats, they'd sail to weather more often."

In Comparison

- Safety-at-sea factor: 14 (Rated against the 19 other boats in this book, with 1 being safest.)
- Speed rating: Reputedly quite fast to weather and good passagemaker.
- Ocean comfort level: One or two adults in comfort.

These, and other, equally glowing opinions come from the sales literature distributed by the Sam L. Morse company. Over the hill? Of course. It's highly regrettable, but you can't find a Falmouth Cutter owner who isn't.

Conclusion

This is a very modern old-fashioned boat, one that retains the best characteristics of traditional design and blends them with the latest boatbuilding technology. If it's true that the best things come in small packages, then the Falmouth Cutter 22 proves the rule.

It also proves the rule that small things are not necessarily inexpensive things. The basic price of a new boat from the factory is $99,000. But, considering what you get for the money, it's good value. And used boats are a lot cheaper, although you rarely come across one on the open market because they're snapped up so quickly and quietly. It's the Falmouth Cutter cult at work, you know. They look after their own.

Chapter Thirteen
Flicka 20

Minimum Cruiser, Maximum Charm

You can't hold a sensible discussion about small seagoing sailboats without mentioning the Flicka 20. Who, you might ask, would willingly pay $60,000 to $70,000 to go to sea on a boat only 20 feet long on deck – about the length of three bathtubs?

The answer to that question is – hundreds of people. At least 400 so far. So the next question is: Why? What's this snub-nosed midget got that makes otherwise rational deepsea sailors haul out their checkbooks and scribble their signatures in mad anticipation? The short answer is that she has charms that become more apparent and more beguiling the closer you get to her. She is also, in many ways, a dream boat. She appeals to the adventurous spirit that erupts in all of us from time to time, even the armchair sailors. She's capable of crossing oceans in safety. She's our magic carpet, ready to waft us to the virgin white sands of desert islands where the palm trees rustle in the gentle trade winds, and warm blue waters murmur against the reef. And yet we can bring her home on a trailer and store her in the garage for winter, if we want. We don't actually *have* to cross an ocean in her. Knowing that she *can* is good enough. That, and knowing that our neighbors at the marina know she can, any time we want her to.

There is also a good deal of reassurance in the fact that the designer of this boat, Bruce Bingham, lived and sailed on her for two years. He and Katy Burke cruised 6,000 miles in a Flicka 20 called *Sabrina*, traveling down the eastern seaboard of the United States and crossing into the Bahamas. But, even before that, *Sabrina* took part in the 200-mile race around Long Island, New York, only four days after she'd been delivered. She came fourth in the cruising class, according to the publicity people at the Pacific Seacraft Corporation (PS), builders of the Flicka. What PS neglects to say is how many entries there were in the cruising class. Four, maybe? No, we're being too cynical. We must give them the benefit of the doubt, and presume the annual race attracts dozens of cruisers. Which means the tiny 20-foot tot is interestingly light on her toes, too, but not exactly fast. According to the handicap ratings, she's 6 seconds a mile slower than the other 20-footer here, the Cal 20. But if you're seriously concerned about 6 seconds a mile it's obvious that you're not fit to own a Flicka yet. Your priorities are wrong. Please have your head examined and come back when you're better.

Basic Design

The art of yacht design lies in intelligent compromise, and if you want to create a lot of space on a short waterline you have to sacrifice looks or performance, or a bit of both.

Bingham took a small chance on performance, a bigger chance on looks, by designing the Flicka with a hefty beam, tall topsides, and a high coachroof. She's tubby and she's boxy, but somehow, although she has all the potential elements of a bathtub toy, she manages to avoid the sort of stomach-churning ugliness that repels you in mid-stride. Perhaps it's because her sterling character shines through her plain-Jane looks. Perhaps it's because she's pug-ugly. Whatever it is, the word that most frequently comes to people's lips is "cute." And in this case, cute on deck translates into palatial accommodations down below, including headroom of 5 feet 11 inches, and three full-sized berths.

She's a heavy-displacement, Bermudian-rigged sloop or cutter (your choice) with a masthead rig and a headsail set from a short bowsprit. Her hull is solid fiberglass and her fiberglass decks are cored with balsa, but there's solid plywood where deck hardware is attached. She is fitted out in the usual PS tradition, that is to say, with no expense spared regarding materials or workmanship. Her bow, like that of the Dana 24, is distinctively plumb. In fact, it is even more than plumb – the very top bends aft slightly, the better to please the eye. Each Flicka, incidentally, has a very fancy curlicue molded in each side of the bow, joined by a cove line to a smaller one at the stern.

She has a full keel that gathers depth increasingly as it sweeps toward the rudder, making her maximum draft just 3 feet 3 inches. Her 1,800 pounds of ballast is encapsulated well forward in the hull and forms about 30 percent of her total displacement of about 6,000 pounds.

The Flicka is well endowed with beam – 8 feet (the same as a Cape Dory 25D) on a waterline of only 18 feet 2 inches – that slows her progress through the water but gives her spacious accommodations and greater initial stability.

In Short

Flicka 20

Designer: Bruce Bingham

LOA: 24 feet 0 inches

LOD: 20 feet 0 inches

LWL: 18 feet 2 inches

Beam: 8 feet 0 inches

Draft: 3 feet 3 inches

Displacement: 6,000 pounds

Sail area: 243 square feet

Ballast: Encapsulated lead, 1,800 pounds

Spars: Painted aluminum

Auxiliary: Outboard or Yanmar 9-hp diesel inboard

Designed as: Pocket ocean cruiser

Her rudder is fixed to the flat transom and keel, a very seamanlike way of doing things. It's strong, simple, easy to get at, and easy to remove for repairs if necessary.

The decks are surrounded by raised bulwarks with a heavy teak caprail – the true sign of a bluewater voyager. The sidedecks are fairly narrow, and cater only for rather restricted access to the mast and foredeck. Luckily, it takes only a couple of steps to get anywhere on this boat.

The self-draining cockpit is small, but adequate for two, and is uncluttered by the mainsheet, whose traveler attaches to the pulpit railing aft. A watertight hatch in the cockpit sole affords excellent access to the optional inboard engine, and a high-capacity manual bilge pump is mounted handy to the helm. The Flicka 20 carries 20 gallons of fresh water in a tank under the quarterberth. You might want to take an extra supply in stowable jugs when you do cross that ocean. The head holding tank has a capacity of 8 gallons, and the diesel fuel tank, which lives up forward under the V-berth, quite divorced from the engine, also holds 8 gallons.

If you have an outboard engine, which is the choice

Flicka 20

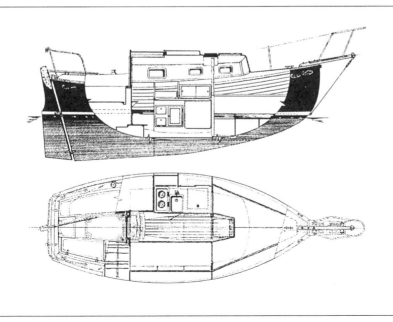

of many Flicka owners, you can use the fuel tank for extra drinking water, of course. You'll also have a lot of extra space aft of the companionway steps.

The standard inboard engine is the ubiquitous Yanmar 1GM10, a single-cylinder diesel of 9 horsepower, fitted with a 35-amp alternator. It's a good match for this boat, and very economical.

Accommodations

As you step below on the Flicka 20 you gain the reward for her "cute" exterior. The interior is absolutely huge for a 20-footer, warm and inviting. PS has used interior molds, bonded to the skin, but has covered much of the white fiberglass with honey-colored, hand-rubbed teak – enough to create an impression of classy workmanship and opulence, but not so much as to turn the interior dark and uninteresting.

The portlights are of solid bronze, and all six of them open to give as much through-ventilation are you're ever likely to need. Overhead, the white vinyl headliner is zipped in place for easy removal.

This is another boat with an open-plan interior; that is to say, there is no bulkhead separating the forepeak from the main cabin. A beefed-up deckbeam takes the thrust of the deck-stepped mast, and apparently passes some of it down to the keel via an off-center compression post at the forward corner of the galley.

The happy result is the appearance of abundant space, starting up forward with the V-berth, whose size obviously benefits from the boat's generous beam. In what would normally be the main cabin, Bingham has provided a settee, a galley with a two-burner stove, a sink, and an icebox, and – wait for it – an enclosed head compartment and hanging locker to starboard of the companionway steps. To port, aft of the galley, is the third full-size berth, a quarterberth running under the cockpit. At sea, this will often be the only habitable berth, of course, but for two people working watch and watch about, that won't cause problems. There may be occasions, however, when both crewmembers are below in heavy weather, and in that case one of them is going to have to sleep on the cabin sole. But that surely a small penalty to pay for owning such a "cute" boat.

The Rig

With spars and sails hardly bigger than a dinghy's, there's nothing complicated about this rig. You can turn the basic sloop into a cutter if you are so disposed, but there really isn't much of an advantage to splitting up such a tiny rig, and there may even be a disadvantage in the extra windage created by the inner forestay and its associated halyard and sheets.

Both mast and boom are made of aluminum, painted with twin-pack polyurethane paint. The mast is stayed at the truck and has a single spreader, from whose roots spring fore lower shrouds and aft lower shrouds on each side. The backstay is made fast to the transom without any need for a bumpkin. All the turnbuckles are of the forged bronze type, with open bodies.

The mainsail has an area of 106 square feet, and the working jib is a little bigger at 137 square feet. The mainsail has two rows of reef points built in, and by the time you've pulled down the second reef there's hardly enough canvas left to blow your nose on. Very snug.

Performance

Almost everything you say about the Flicka 20 has to be qualified by the phrase "for her size." She's dry for her size. She's reasonably stiff for her size. She's quite fast for her size. But you have to remember that her size is small.

Her generous freeboard will certainly keep her decks dry when she's running or reaching, but when she's driving to windward in heavy weather she will quickly start the spray flying aft to the cockpit.

It's not her fault. She's only little.

Similarly, her beam makes her stiff for a 20-footer, but she's not going to be able to fly all her working sail in 25 knots, as a Folkboat might. And while her initial stability is comparatively good, her ultimate stability cannot match that of a Contessa or a Nicholson 32.

It really doesn't help much to compare this boat with others. Her performance depends on where you take her and how you sail her. "Long passages of a 5-knot average and better are not uncommon," says the PS brochure. Well, you can't ask for much better than that. And if you count interior space and comfort as a measure of cruising performance, as you should, the Flicka suddenly emerges into a realm of her own.

Besides, Flicka owners "tend to be independent and thoughtful" according to the observant staff at Pacific Seacraft. Just the kind of sailors who don't give a damn what anybody else thinks about their boats, good or bad.

Known Weaknesses

• Smallness. Size is not the major factor in seaworthiness, and a small boat used with commonsense and great caution can be reasonably safe at sea. Nevertheless, it would be foolhardy to attempt to cross an ocean in a boat as small as this without a solid knowledge of sailing and a fair amount of experience. That said, it must acknowledged that many boats less seaworthy than the Flicka have crossed oceans, and even sailed around the world. In the long run, it's the combination of boat and sailor that counts.

• The difficulty of carrying a shore tender. Even a rolled-up inflatable takes up a lot of room below on a boat this size.

• Despite her wide beam, owners report that she's quite tender initially. She'll quickly heel over to about 15 degrees, and then stubbornly dig right in.

• The stove is not gimbaled.

Owner's Opinion

Probably the most famous owner of a Flicka 20 is John Welch, who is retired and lives in Hawaii. He has sailed *Betty Jane* from California to Hawaii, and from Hawaii to Tahiti and back. He has also made a trip from Hawaii to Palmyra Island.

During the outward trip to Palmyra he experienced fine weather with steady northeasterly winds of 20 to 25 knots. *Betty Jane* wore her best working clothes with one

> ### In Comparison
> • Safety-at-sea factor: 17 (Rated against the 19 other boats in this book, with 1 being safest.)
> • Speed rating: Not fast. Reputed PHRF rating 300.
> • Ocean comfort level: One or two adults in comfort, at least for most of the time.

reef in the main most of the way, and flew along under perfect balance. Her best day's run was 123 miles and she managed to average more than 100 miles day over the whole passage.

But the return trip to Hawaii was another matter altogether. "In one day it would go from becalmed to 45-knot squalls," Welch recalls, "absolutely the most adverse weather conditions possible." It made for a lot of work and many sail changes, but the Flicka never gave him pause for concern. "She really proved herself," he says.

Tom Messick also is the famous owner of a Flicka 20, but he's famous for a different reason. He and his teenage daughter, Mitzi, went aground in their boat, *Tondelayo*, during a lightning storm in Tampa Bay, Florida.

After pounding on the sands of Egmont Key in fading light, *Tondelayo* was swept into the Gulf of Mexico and fetched up in the surf several hundred yards short of the ruins of an old fort. For hours the Flicka pounded in the surf on an incoming tide, lashed by steady rain driven by a 40-knot wind.

"Finally the lightning abated and we went on deck," Messick said. "We were able, in time, to turn her bow away from the beach. With the winch and the engine we slowly began to make some progress, but we were paying an agonizing price as she would gain a foot, and then slam hard on the bottom again. In about an hour we finally came free."

Messick motored *Tondelayo* to an anchorage, checking the bilge all the way, but discovered it was bone dry. "I could hardly believe my eyes," he said. At first light he checked for underwater damage and found nothing structural – just some scratch marks on the paint.

He summed up his experience succinctly: "I have to conclude that our Flicka is one very tough lady."

Conclusion

The Flicka is high quality in a small package with a large price tag. But you have to remember that she offers the accommodations (if not the performance) of a boat 6 or 8 feet longer. For a cruising couple, that's snug but ample.

Because she is a cult boat, and because she is strongly and sensibly constructed, the Flicka retains her value very well on the second-hand market. She ages well, and there is very little to go wrong. The price of a used Flicka will be substantially lower than that of a new boat, of course, but there are very few basement bargains unless you happen to come across one of the pre-1978 originals, built by an amateur from a finished hull or a kit.

Flickas built by Pacific Seacraft are rugged, solid craft, with top-quality cabinetry, finish, and detailing. There isn't another production boat of her size in the U.S. that rivals her interior space and ocean-going capabilities. She's small enough to handle easily, but big enough to live in comfortably.

For the price of a new Flicka, you could buy a used larger boat of another make, just as seaworthy and a whole lot faster and more comfortable. Hundreds of Flicka owners know that full well, but they're not tempted. This little spellbinder is all they've ever sought, and all they'll ever need.

Chapter Fourteen
The Folkboat

Little Beauty with a Big Heart

Tord Sunden's Nordic Folkboat is a sailing legend. She was one of the few items of exceptional merit to emerge from the horror years of 1939-1945 when much of the world was experiencing the convulsions of war.

Sunden's home country was Sweden, which had declared neutrality in World War II, and in the early 1940s the Swedes organized an international competition for a new common Scandinavian class of sailboats. The organizers were looking for a cheap, fast, seaworthy, one-design racing boat that could also be used for family cruising during weekends and holidays.

Nearly 60 designs were entered for the competition, but none was accepted outright, and Tord Sunden, then an amateur yacht designer, was chosen by the organizing committee to pull together the most promising aspects of the top four designs submitted.

The result was the nautical equivalent of the German Volkswagen, the people's car. She was named the people's boat, the Folkboat. But little did the organizers of the competition imagine how successful she would be. Eighty orders poured in from all over Sweden before the final plans were completed.

Today, 60 or so years after the first Nordic Folkboat was launched, there are thousands of Folkboats afloat, wooden ones and fiberglass ones. The majority are in Europe, with Sweden leading the pack, followed by Denmark, Germany, Finland, and the United Kingdom. There are about 120 in San Francisco, where the San Francisco Bay Folkboat Association administers the fleet, and where the Folkboat's wonderful heavy-weather performance is much admired.

Besides the Nordic Folkboats, all of which comply with the class's one-design rules, there are thousands of near-Folkboats, close look-alikes such as the Contessa 26, most of which attempt to increase her interior living space with more beam, a longer waterline, and a larger coachroof, while retaining her fabled seakeeping qualities and her classical good looks.

In 1966, Tord Sunden introduced a variant of the classic Nordic Folkboat that lacked the traditional lapstrake planking. It was carvel-planked and featured a shallower, self-bailing cockpit. She also was more luxurious below. She was known as the International Folkboat, but the Scandinavians regarded that description as misleading, and referred to her only as the "IF Boat." The term International Folkboat survived in the United States, however, and the International Folkboat Association of San Francisco

Bay held sway over their racing and cruising activities there.

Basic Design

The original design concept had a long, overhanging stern, like a 30-Square-Meter's. But that was later chopped off, probably because a long overhang adds considerably to building costs. The result was a much more seaworthy transom stern. The transom, however, was given a handsome rake so it would better match the moderate overhang of the bow, and thus the after end of the full keel also was clipped away to line up with it. That, together with the generous cutaway up forward, greatly reduced the wetted area of the keel without affecting its efficiency. Early critics thought the raked rudder would make steering difficult under some circumstances, but experience proved them wrong.

The first boats were, of course, built of wood. Their hulls were clinker-built, or of lapstrake construction, with each strake overlapping the upper edge of its neighbor below. This makes the boat strong and light. It also adds greatly to her looks by repeating and emphasizing the sweet lines of her sheer. The first fiberglass Nordic Folkboats were legalized in 1977, and were exact reproductions of the wooden boat, including the overlapping strakes. They raced on equal terms with wooden boats and were forced by the strict one-design rules to use wooden masts.

The International Folkboats were regarded as a separate class, although their overall measurements and design were basically the same. They, too, were produced in fiberglass, but with smooth topsides and lighter aluminum masts.

Between 1967 and 1984, when production ceased, Marieholms Bruk, of Sweden, launched more than 3,400 International Folkboats, hitting an annual record high of 552 boats in 1975. After that, there was a steep decline in demand, although almost 1,000 were sold in the next nine years.

Production of fiberglass Nordic boats also continued apace, and a Danish boatbuilder, Folkebådcentralen A/S, of Kerteminde, has now built more than 900 Nordic Folkboats that are solid GRP replicas of the original wooden-hulled design, lapped strakes and all. The Folkboat has a rounded underbody with fairly slack bilges, a combination that makes for slight initial tenderness but more than compensates for it with comfort at sea. After that initial tilt, she stiffens up considerably, so much so that she is able to race in winds strong enough to keep other classes in port. The topsides and the cabintop are low, offering little resistance to the wind and making no concessions to creature comfort below. The foredeck is uncluttered – there are only a hatch and a mooring cleat to stub your toes on – and convenient to work on.

The cockpit is a compromise between the needs of racers and cruisers – barely big enough for a racing crew, barely small enough for serious deepsea cruising. Some Folkboats have a deep cockpit that is more sheltered and more comfortable, but it drains into the bilge. Serious deepsea sailors will want the other version, a self-bailing cockpit that will not endanger the ship if it fills with water. The rudder hangs outboard of the transom, a simple, strong and easily accessible arrangement. The tiller sweeps across the after deck, but doesn't interfere much with the crew in the cockpit.

The engine is a matter of choice and depends on whether your boat is Nordic or International. Some boats have a well in the cockpit for an outboard motor of between 5 hp and 8 hp. Others mount an outboard on the transom. Still others prefer an inboard

The Folkboat

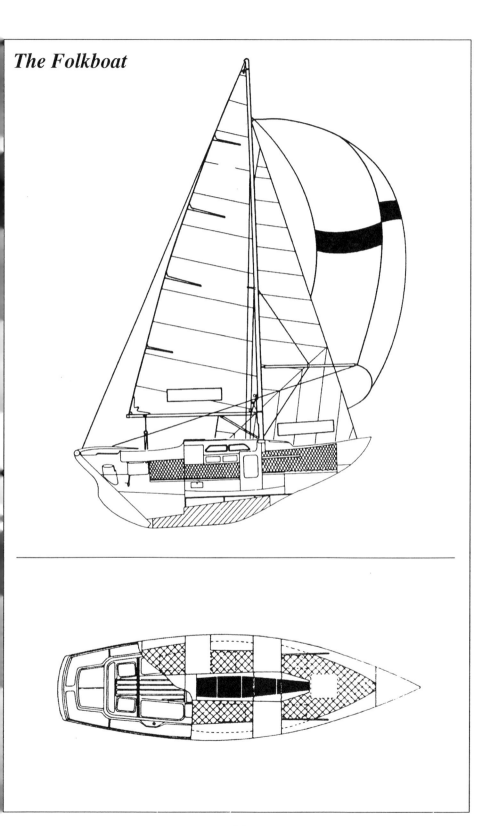

auxiliary, usually a single-cylinder diesel. If you're planning an ocean crossing in a Folkboat, it would make a lot of sense to choose an outboard, and to keep it on the transom. If you find it interferes with your self-steering gear, you may have to house it in a well, in which case you can either leave it down, causing a little drag in the water, or remove it and store it below while you're on passage. The inboard engine makes more sense for weekenders or coastal cruisers who won't miss the valuable stowage space as much as the bluewater cruisers will.

Accommodations

It doesn't take long to describe the Folkboat's accommodations, although they, too, can vary according to whether she's Nordic or IF, and from builder to builder. On the IF boats there's usually teak everywhere, and vinyl headliners. The hull is lined with padded vinyl, too, in place of wooden ceiling. The V-berth has two berths more than 6 feet long, and the main cabin has two settee berths, even longer. Some boats have an enclosed head compartment, and others are supplied with a portable head. There's a rudimentary galley, and there may even be a small chart table. There's usually a hanging locker somewhere, and a few lockers and shelves scattered around the place, though not nearly enough for a long voyage. Nowhere is there sufficient room to swing a cat, and nowhere is the headroom more than 4 feet 8 inches.

The interior is bright and airy, though, especially with the companionway sliding hatch open, and seems very welcoming and protected in contrast to the exposed conditions of the cockpit.

The Rig

The Nordic Folkboat is a Bermudian sloop with a wooden mast and a conspicuous fractional rig – the forestay joins the mast about two-thirds of the way up from the deck. This makes for a small working jib and a large mainsail. It is, perhaps, not as efficient as a rig with a larger jib, seeing that the jib does most of the work when going to windward, but it certainly makes for happier cockpit crews when the load on the jib sheets is small.

Folkboats not subject to the one-design racing rules usually have modern masthead rigs and aluminum spars. Many of the boats in the United States are rigged that way. If you're more interested in crossing oceans than in racing around the buoys the aluminum masthead rig might be preferable because it makes provision for double lower shrouds in place of the single after lower shroud that is standard on wooden masts.

The mast is stepped on deck but appears to be well supported by a massive deck beam and seems not to compress the cabin top as so many others do. Presumably, after more than 50 years of racing and ocean cruising, the

---

In Short

Folkboat

Designer: Tord Sunden (1942)

LOA: 25 feet 1 inch

LWL: 19 feet 8 inches

Beam: 7 feet 2 inches

Draft: 3 feet 11 inches

Displacement: 4,322 pounds

Sail area: 258 square feet

Ballast: Cast iron, 2,315 pounds

Spars: Wood/aluminum

Auxiliary: Outboard or inboard, gasoline or diesel

Designed as: One-design family racer/cruiser

Note: These dimensions were supplied by Folkebådcentralen A/S, in Kerteminde, Denmark, builders of the fiberglass Nordic Folkboat.

builders of Folkboats have got it right. Right from the beginning, Nordic Folkboat owners agreed to race without spinnakers, to make thing easier for family sailors and shorthanded crews. But those gung-ho Finns couldn't stand it. Even though they couldn't compete internationally with spinnakers, they raced with them among themselves.

"We simply think that sailing with a spinnaker is more fun, and that it makes sailing more colorful," explained a member of the Finnish Folkboat Association.

Performance

Any class that is still going strong after more than 50 years obviously has something good going for it. The Folkboat has several excellent features, not the least of which is her performance. For a full-keel boat, she is surprisingly fast and close-winded. Her PHRF rating is 228 for boats with outboard engines, and 234 for boats with inboards.

On top of that, she's easy to handle. A picture of IF Boat 377 (*Magnificent Obsession*) published in *Latitude 38* magazine in June, 1998, shows her rail-down just outside San Francisco's Golden Gate in 25 knots and more. She has one reef in the mainsail and full working jib – and her tiller is being held dead fore-and-aft. No weather helm there.

The Folkboat is indeed revered for her ability to carry sail in strong winds, and no doubt her extra-heavy keel is largely responsible for this. The ballast ratio is an extraordinary 54 percent, which means the iron keel alone weighs more than all the rest of the boat. Little wonder that Folkboats were, and still are, so popular in the blustery San Francisco Bay area. Her performance as a seaboat is legendary, of course. It wasn't just a coincidence that two of the six boats in the first Singlehanded Transatlantic Race, in 1960, were Folkboats. Valentine Howells raced in the conventional Folkboat *Eira*, while Colonel H. G. ("Blondie") Hasler sailed a much-modified Folkboat, the famous *Jester*, which had a standard hull but a flush deck with a central control point and a Chinese lug rig.

The long keel gives the Folkboat good directional stability, and this, together with her zesty performance and her easy motion, makes her a sensible choice for a singlehanded voyager or a young couple – and we say a young couple only because young people are more likely to be forgiving about the Folkboat's biggest disadvantage, her lack of interior space.

Known Weaknesses

After nearly 60 years of production and real-life testing, there are no weaknesses left in the Folkboat that are not patently obvious, such as the cramped accommodation quarters. This is a very open, honest boat.

If you're contemplating buying one for a long voyage, you'll have to look for the wear and tear applicable to boats in general. Inspect the hull for the dreaded boat pox, if she's GRP, and be careful to locate any areas of rot if she's wooden. Dance on those fiberglass decks and tap away with your screwdriver handle. As always, even if you think you know it all, it's a wise move to get a second opinion. Let a qualified surveyor check her out. It's your life that's at stake.

Owner's Opinions

This is another boat people fall in love with so passionately that it's difficult to get an owner to say a word against a Folkboat. Her classic beauty alone is enough to still all criticism.

Yet the physical exploits of her devotees give us valuable insights into her abilities when the sole arbiter is the sea itself. Blondie Hasler's wooden *Jester* is both a good and a bad example of this. Good, because she crossed the Atlantic 14 times. Bad, because she was eventually lost at sea without trace. But she was very old and she had suffered more punishment than a dozen normal boats.

From the waterline down, *Jester* was a normal Folkboat, but the rest of her had been greatly modified by her owner, who was much given to invention and experimentation. She was a very early model, and in fact sailed from 1952 to 1959 with Hasler's "lapwing" rig before he threw that out and installed a junk rig for the 1960 Observer Singlehanded Transatlantic Race.

Hasler came in second in that race, a remarkable achievement. He was only eight days behind Francis Chichester's *Gipsy Moth III,* a much bigger and faster 39-foot sloop that crossed the finish line 40 days after the start. *Jester* was driven hard, and was reduced in one gale to what Hasler described as "four reefs down."

The other Folkboat in that race, *Eira,* came in fourth out of six in 63 days. *Eira* was knocked on her beam ends, and Valentine Howells put into Bermuda to replace a chronometer he had lost and to repair some damage.

In 1963, Adrian Hayter circumnavigated the world alone, sailing halfway – from England to New Zealand – in *Sheila II,* a 32-footer. But he completed the New Zealand-to-England leg in a Folkboat called *Valkyr.* Mike Bale also sailed from England to New Zealand in a Folkboat called *Jellicle,* and had a crew for part of the way. In 1975, a 55-year-old Australian grandmother called Ann Gash sailed around the world singlehanded in a Folkboat called *Ilimo.* She chose the east-to-west route via the Panama Canal, but had the boat shipped for part of the way, from Ghana to England.

More recently, a British Folkboat called *Storm Petrel* was completing an unusual circumnavigation in 1998 with solo sailor Tony Curphey aboard. It was unusual because Tony's wife, Suzanne, was also making a singlehanded circumnavigation aboard her own boat, a 30-foot Seadog ketch called *Glory.* They had originally set out separately, not knowing each other, but they met in New Zealand and got married in the Solomon Islands.

Tony's Folkboat often beat Suzanne's Seadog into port on subsequent legs of their tandem voyage and regularly clocked up 130 miles a day in the trade winds. Their plan, once they had completed their solo circumnavigations, was to sell their boats, buy a bigger one, and carry on cruising – but together this time. There are undoubtedly many other Folkboats that have sailed around the world and around Cape Horn, singlehanded and crewed, whose names have not been recorded in the annals of small boat sailing. There was a time, 50 years ago, when such voyages were rare, and records were kept of individual exploits. Now that they are more commonplace, nobody seems to be keeping the tally, which is a great pity. Perhaps the Internet will one day find place for the Roll of Honor of smallboat circumnavigations; if it does, the Folkboat will surely feature prominently.

Conclusion

According to Marek Janiec, a member of the Swedish International Folkboat (IF) Association's technical committee, there are about 2,000 IFs in Sweden, and the market price there for a boat in excellent condition is about 60,000 Swedish kroner, or $7,400 U.S. There are about 4,000 IF Boats scattered throughout the globe, which makes it the biggest deep-keel racing class in the world. "In Denmark, the price is 20 percent to 30 percent higher, and down in Europe, still 20 percent more." So – would you score a financial coup by going to Sweden, buying a cheap Folkboat, and sailing her home? Probably not, although it's a very attractive plan in any case. Second-hand International Folkboats sell on the West Coast of the United States for between $10,000 and $14,000, so the savings are not substantial in actual dollar terms if you factor in travel and accommodation charges. A brand-new fiberglass Nordic Folkboat costs about $40,000 in Denmark.

In Comparison

- Safety-at-sea factor: 9 (Rated against the 19 other boats in this book, with 1 being safest.)
- Speed rating: Fast for her size and displacement.
- Ocean comfort level: One or two adults in fairly cramped conditions. ("If you want to stand up," said the famous British designer Uffa Fox, "go on deck.")

Wherever you buy one, a Folkboat represents good value for a boat capable of carrying one or two people around the world, albeit in cramped surroundings. Besides that, if you have any finer feelings at all you'll have to agree that she's one of the most beautiful boats ever made to go to sea. Just looking at her riding to anchor in her own reflection in a tropical lagoon will make your heart leap with delight.

Chapter Fifteen
Frances 26/Morris 26

They Roam the World's Oceans

The British manufacturers of Frances 26 sloops manage to characterize them perfectly in remarkably few words: "They routinely roam the world's oceans." Enough said, old chap. In fact, the Frances 26 has an Anglo-American heritage, for she was designed by one of America's best-known smallboat architects, Chuck Paine.

Morris Yachts, of Maine, originally built the Frances as the Morris 26 – about 35 to 40 of them came off the production line there – and you can still order the Frances through them. In total, about 200 have so far been constructed professionally, and about 40 more have been built by amateurs from sets of plans – still available, incidentally, from Chuck Paine's design office in Camden, Maine.

For all her workmanlike appearance, this tough little double-ender now built by Victoria Yachts, in Hampshire, England, is an upscale sailboat, built exclusively to order for about $80,000. That's about $12 per pound of displacement – expensive, but still cheaper than some. Building to order means you can have the interior altered to your own desire (within reason) at no extra cost. Thus, you gain the benefits of a near-custom design at the price of a production boat.

Significantly, the Frances 26 was designed by Chuck Paine for his own use. She was, in fact, his first design as an independent naval architect, and she had to be capable of cruises from Maine to the West Indies and back, crossing the unpredictable Gulf Stream. She also had to be capable of being sailed by only one or two persons.

For his own comfort and safety, Paine chose a traditional, long-keeled hull with moderately heavy displacement, an outboard rudder, and short ends. It's interesting that so many designers who plan to cross oceans in their own boats choose that time-tested formula, no matter how many fancy fin-and skeg boats they draw for others.

This boat is almost a starved Colin Archer, except that her sternpost is straight, not curved, and that the forward end of her keel is cut away slightly, for better maneuverability, less drag, and better directional stability downwind. Paine says that the cutaway also stops her from developing weather helm.

Although many of these small voyagers are now routinely roaming the world's oceans, and although their numbers are growing all the time, you won't often find many used ones for sale on the open market. At the time of writing, Morris Yachts was advertising four for sale from $38,000 upward, but this is the kind of boat owners tend to hang on to for life, and when they do come up for sale they're quickly snapped up by savvy sailors who've been waiting in the wings for their chance to pounce.

Better get in line.

Basic Design

One unusual aspect of this boat's design is the amount of weight she carries on her keel. The ratio of ballast to displacement is 51 percent. In other words, more than half the total weight of the boat resides in her ballast keel. Such a high ratio is rarely seen in a cruising boat, but it augurs well for her ultimate stability. Should she ever be rolled over by a rogue wave (and that possibility should never be dismissed, no matter the size of the yacht) she will undoubtedly regain her feet very swiftly, probably before too much water has found its way down below. Her hull is solid, hand-laid fiberglass, built to Lloyd's specification with the gelcoat colored according to the owner's choice. The fiberglass deck has a core of balsa wood except in those places where fittings are bolted through – there the core is more substantial material known (appropriately enough) as coremat.

Each end of the hull is pointed and joined by a full-length keel of traditional proportions, modified slightly (as if the designer were making a nodding concession to modernity) by removing a thin crescent from its forward edge.

The freeboard is generous but cunningly lessened visually by what the builders call a "gunwale styling line." And yes, she has proper gunwales, capped by a solid teak toerail.

Her coachroof is high, angular, and truncated. It stops short of the mast, and by rights ought to look unflatteringly boxy. For some reason, though (perhaps because of its deep crown or the shape of its ports) it earns the epithet "purposeful" rather than the disparagement "ugly." In any case, it provides full standing headroom in the main cabin below, which is no mean trick on a 26-footer. This is one of the last remaining boats provided with the cruiser's friend, a proper Samson post on the foredeck. Nothing is more convenient for mooring lines, anchor lines, and towing lines, yet fewer and fewer modern sailors ever get the chance to test its virtues against the inadequately sized and awkwardly placed deck cleat that has become the mediocre standard. The sliding hatch over the companionway is made of 3/8-inch thick acrylic plastic material. It slides on brass runners inside a fiberglass turtle, or sea hood, that prevents heavy water from finding its way under the hatch into the accommodations. Teak coamings surround the modestly sized, self-bailing cockpit, which has a vented locker for propane gas and a large lazarette aft. The tiller sweeps the aft end of the cockpit, but without getting in the way too much. A more inconvenient obstacle is the mainsheet, which attaches to a deadeye on the bridgedeck. Even at the cost of some efficiency, the mainsheet might better be sheeted to a horse spanning the pulpit, as it was on the original *Frances*.

You'll find all kinds of power plants in the Frances, ranging from 5 hp to 25 hp, but the standard engine is a diesel, the freshwater-cooled Volvo twin 2010, which develops 10 horsepower. That's slightly more power than the 3 horsepower per ton often recommended for modern cruisers, but it certainly won't be too much in heavy weather.

Victoria Yachts commendably goes to some trouble to reduce noise by lining the engine compartment with an insulating foam that incorporates a lead barrier.

Francis 26/
Morris 26

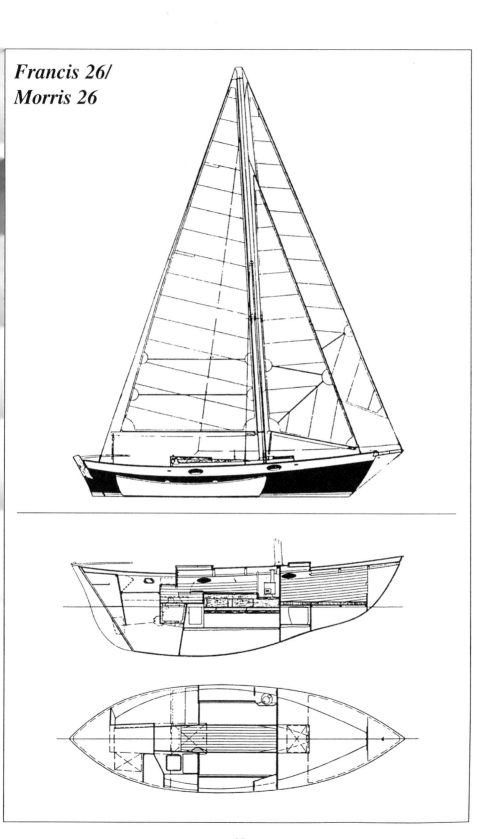

Accommodations

Since most of these boats have been built to the requirements of individual owners, who knows what you might find down below? Their coachroofs, or lack of them, reflect the status quo in the eternal battle between the hedonists, who insist on comfort below, and the Spartans, who are happy to suffer for good looks. A handful of Franceses were built with a raised deck amidships. They are very sleek, very pretty, but they offer no standing headroom below. They make Spartans very happy indeed.

The majority have a raised coachroof to open up the accommodations, and while some of them have a jaunty, truncated cabintop (an uneasy truce, but acceptable to both armies) others have a coachroof that extends forward of the mast in total surrender to the hedonists.

If you're buying a new boat, there's wonderful scope for designing your own interior. If you very sensibly decide that four berths are two too many for this boat, you can get rid of those rarely-used V-berths and put something more useful in their place. And if you simply can't live without a double berth in which to commit connubial bliss, it's easy to make an extension berth from one of the settees in the saloon.

The galley, the head, and the chart table, like moveable feasts, are to be found all over the place on various boats. If you like jig-saw puzzles, you could have a lot of fun planning your own arrangements and offering them to the builder to be shot down in flames.

You can, in fact, squeeze four full-sized berths into this hull and still have room for all the rest, but if you're planning to sail singlehanded – or doublehanded, as the majority of long-term cruisers do – you'd be foolish to pass over this opportunity to tailor-make the boat for yourself.

If you truly can't be bothered, Victoria Yachts will be delighted to build you one of their two standard layouts, the Classic, for the short cabintop, and the "800" for the elongated trunk. They'll do it very nicely, too, in a blend of solid teak, teak-veneered plywood, plastic laminate, and panels of light-colored hardwood in strip planks.

The Rig

The rig is another area in which choices abound. You can have a masthead sloop, a 7/8ths-rigged sloop, or a cutter with a bowsprit. You can probably order a wooden mast, if you want – and there are still some advantages to that – but there are perfectly good aluminum spars available that won't need 10 coats of varnish every season.

Victoria Yachts supplies a thoroughly modern, silver-anodized mast, stepped on deck, with airfoil spreaders and an internal conduit to stop those electrical wires slapping around inside the mast and driving you crazy. In a typically thoughtful touch, they even supply a drawline, or messenger line, so you don't have to call a professional electrician to feed your wires through the conduit.

The boom, also silver-anodized, has a built-in groove for the mainsail foot boltrope and an internal reefing system for two slab reefs. There's a special winch to aid jiffy reefing, and a fancy casting near the gooseneck with four built-in jammers for the reef lines and the clew downhaul.

The sail area, incidentally, is exactly 30 square meters, or 327 square feet, with a slight majority of it in the mainsail so that the headsails can more easily be managed by shorthanded crews. If you're familiar with the old International 30-Square Meter class, you, too, will be fascinated by the fact that the exact same sail area that drives those glamorous but malnourished 40-foot racers so quickly and efficiently is needed to push the sturdy Frances 26 along in rather more prosaic fashion.

Performance

This is a seakindly boat, as comfortable in broken water as any 26-footer can be expected to be, and more seaworthy than most. Her pointed stern will win the approval of many traditionalists who believe that it parts following seas as does the stern of a lifeboat, and thus makes the hull more seaworthy. Even those who scoff at such a theory on the grounds that if a big wave is going to come over the stern, a pointed end won't stop it, must agree that is it pretty to look at.

Her performance to windward will depend to some extent on the chosen rig: a masthead sloop with a hanked-on foresail will probably do best because the size of the headsail is important. It is simply more efficient than the mainsail, area for area, because it is not affected by the power-wasting vortices spawned by the mast.

She's a little shallow-drafted for premium performance on the wind, so she'll need to be sailed a bit freer and a bit more upright in heavy sea conditions, but in light or moderate weather she might surprise a few competitors. Like most full-keel boats, she comes into her own as you ease her off the wind, and there's no reason why she shouldn't notch up some pretty respectable daily runs on an ocean passage.

Known Weaknesses

• Expense. New or used, this is not a cheap boat. If she's well maintained though, she could make a safe, solid investment because there always seem to be more people looking for used boats of this type than there are examples available.

• Lack of availability. If you want a used one, you'll probably find there are fewer than half-a-dozen for sale in the United States at any one time. You may have to track one down and haunt the owner until he or she sells it to you.

Owner's Opinion

In this case, the owner's opinion is the designer's, too. Chuck Paine's original *Frances*, named for a friend in London, had a 7/8th sloop rig for no better reason than the fact that it looked pretty. For the same reason, she also had a flush deck instead of a raised cabintop.

He calls her a mid-Atlantic boat. "I wanted to combine the qualities of the best of British and American design," he said, and she has, in fact, appealed to people on both sides of the Atlantic."

He designed her as a deepsea voyager with

> ### In Short
> **Frances 26/Morris 26**
> Designer: Chuck Paine
> LOA: 26 feet 0 inches
> LWL: 21 feet 3 inches
> Beam: 8 feet 2 inches
> Draft: 3 feet 10 inches
> Displacement:
> 6,800 pounds
> Sail area: 327 square feet
> Ballast: 3,500 pounds
> Spars: Anodized aluminum
> Auxiliary: Volvo 10 hp
>   diesel
> Designed as: Easily
>   managed ocean
>   voyager

ruggedness, character, and good looks. She had to be small enough to suit a modest budget, but large enough to survive at sea. But it was Paine's concern with seaworthiness that was paramount. That's one of the reasons he gave her a whopping 51-percent ballast ratio."

She has very positive capsize numbers," he said, "She can heel a very long way over before she reaches her limit of positive stability."

> ## In Comparison
>
> - Safety-at-sea factor: 10 (Rated against the 19 other boats in this book, with 1 being safest.)
> - Speed rating: An efficient performer but best on a reach.
> - Ocean comfort level: One or two adults in reasonable comfort.

To the uninitiated it may seem paradoxical, but despite all this weight hanging from her keel, *Frances* is a little tender initially. Many of the most seaworthy yachts share this tendency to heel quite easily to 10 or 15 degrees, and then suddenly stiffen up, refusing to heel further until the wind really starts to blow seriously. The reward for this lack of initial stability is increased ultimate stability, a feature that should be borne in mind by every prospective ocean sailor. If she's ever hurled upside down by a giant wave, *Frances* will bob upright again very promptly. A very stiff boat, one that gains her initial stability from wide beam, will take much longer to recover, and may even sink before she does.

You don't have to worry about the cockpit being too big on this boat, either. "It's small," said Paine, "it's safe for ocean cruising."

If you're sailing a sloop-rigged *Frances* under all plain sail when the wind starts to rise, you should first reef the mainsail, he advised. If you're sailing the cutter, however, with a roller furling headsail on the bowsprit, you should roll up the Yankee completely and hang on to the staysail.

The idea is to lessen her angle of heel as much as to keep her helm balanced. In fact, *Frances* does not seem to suffer from weather helm. "She's the most beautifully balanced boat of her type that I have ever sailed," Paine said, throwing modesty to the winds.

"She's not as bad to windward as you might suspect, either, specially in moderate weather, but her best point of sail is a reach, anything from a close reach to a broad reach. Dead downwind, like any small boat of this type, she rolls."

Conclusion

There are very few boats that you can have built largely to your own design these days, unless you are rich beyond the dreams of avarice, but the Frances 26/Morris 26 is one of them. Like many a jewel, she's costly for her size but brings a great deal of pleasure for a very long time. Even if money is an object, there are very good reasons for buying this sweet but tough little boat. You could, after all, spend a lot more on a bigger boat that would get you no farther and give you a lot more trouble

Chapter Sixteen
Nicholson 31

No Compromises in This Powerful Cruiser

The Nicholson 31 is a deceptive boat. Above the waterline she has the lines of a sleek modern racer/cruiser. Her cabintop is low and streamlined, with elongated Eurostyle portlights and aluminum-framed hatches. Her bow protrudes forward enough to give her an appearance of constant movement. Her no-nonsense stern is clipped off short and businesslike and her tall masthead sloop rig looks powerful and efficient.

But below the boot-topping it's another story altogether. She lies deep in the water and her full-length keel is cut away in the forefoot in the modern fashion. Her long rudder hangs outboard from the transom and the keel, and her tiller pokes through an elongated slot in the aft cockpit coaming. You begin to realize that this is no club racer/ weekend cruiser after all. There are no compromises here. This is all pure cruiser/ cruiser. And not a bowsprit, a bumpkin, or a bit of baggywrinkle in sight.

She is the replacement for another dedicated cruiser, the Nicholson 32, which went out of production in the late 1970s. The 32 was a landmark boat for the British boatbuilding industry because she had ushered the venerable boatbuilding firm of Camper & Nicholson into the era of the fiberglass production boat in the 1960s. Before that, for two centuries or more, Camper & Nicholsons had produced only one-off, wooden boats, usually a lot larger than 32 feet.

At first, the fiberglass hulls of the 32s were fitted out entirely in wood, but in the very latter part of their highly successful production run, which went through 11 "marks," the 32s started receiving plastic liners and molds for the accommodations, trimmed with teak to detract from their sterility. But by the mid-1970s the Nicholson 32 was beginning to look dated with her springy sheerline, low freeboard, long overhangs, and that protruding doghouse in the aft end of the coachroof.

The Nicholson 31, therefore, was born with plastic liners, upgraded construction methods, great new looks, and a drastically modified keel, so she really represented the first of Camper & Nicholson's "modern" plastic boats.

Her construction befits her design intent. She is strong and efficient without any show of ostentation. The real deceit is that while she looks so clubby and racy in such a non-flashy way, this is actually a boat fit to go anywhere. The Nicholson 31 is a true Cape Horner.

Basic Design
The 31 is a heavy-displacement ocean cruiser with a single spreader masthead sloop rig.

She's quite beamy, although not excessively so by today's standards, and has a healthy draft with her ballast carried low down. Her midship sections show a fairly tight turn to the bilges, which speaks of form stiffness additional to that provided by the beam.

Her ballast is molded lead, a 5,300-pound chunk of it glued into the hull's keel cavity and glassed over on top. It gives her a ballast ratio of 33 percent.

Because of her displacement of nearly 15,000 pounds, her interior is voluminous for a 31-footer and she is able to offer full standing headroom without having to resort to a high cabintop that could be vulnerable to damage in heavy seas. You can see from the words "Camper & Nicholson 31" molded into the gelcoat of her stern quarters that this hull is made in two halves and later joined down the middle. The nameplate is situated on a stretch of tumblehome that disguises the boxiness of the topsides and at the same time adds great strength to the hull, but you'd never be able to pop that shape out of a single female mold.

As a matter of interest, Camper & Nicholson didn't make the hulls of their 31s anyway. That job was contracted out to the specialist firm Halmatic, and C&N finished them off and fitted them out.

The hull is solid fiberglass and is reinforced with the kind of foam-filled longitudinal stringers that are missing, but badly needed, on some other makes of so-called ocean cruisers. The coachroof, the cabin sides, and the decks are fiberglass, cored with balsa.

The sidedecks are wide enough to move about on easily, even when the boat is heeled, and the foredeck is clean and uncluttered, thanks to the enclosed anchor locker, which is capacious enough to hide a 35-pound CQR as well as an anchor winch and a hefty pair of mooring bitts.

If you ever need to be convinced that the Nicholson 31 was designed for rugged cruising, take a look at her stemhead fitting. To call it massive would be an understatement. Apart from anything else, two solid bronze rollers almost the size of golf-cart wheels are encased in a flak-proof jacket of stainless steel that must weigh as much as Jenny Craig's worst failure. The cockpit is more than 6 feet long and it's deep, so that the seats seem to have unusually high backs and tend to isolate you from the water. Many people will prefer a higher seating position, and one that affords a better view forward, but there's no denying that you're well protected in there, especially as the forward part of the cockpit is covered by a full-width dodger that comes as a standard fitting.

The cockpit floor is unusual in that part of it is the top of the 25-gallon diesel fuel tank. The real cockpit sole is a teak grating that keeps you from walking on the tank. It's a self-bailing cockpit, of course, and a really efficient one at that.

Two large drains simply exit through the transom above the waterline, so there's never any worry about drain hoses going bad (or their clips rusting away) and flooding the boat. Top-hinged flap valves fixed to the outside of the transom prevent following waves washing back up into the cockpit.

A single propane bottle finds a home in a special locker that drains into the cockpit, but it would make sense to do some modifications here so you could stow at least two 10-pound bottles for a long cruise.

To port, the cockpit seat lifts up to reveal a cavernous sail locker, which should

Nicholson 31

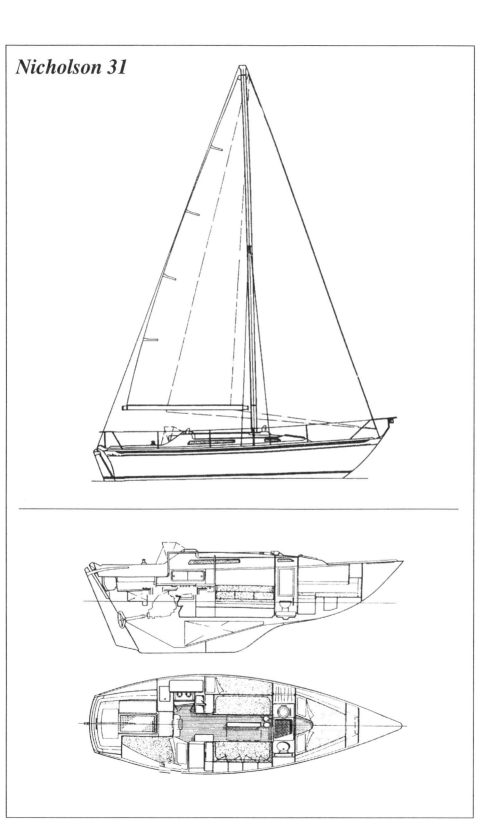

help keep the V-berth clear for its intended use; a catchment area for soiled underwear, orphan socks, and old shackles that have lost their pins.

The standard engine is a three-cylinder Yanmar diesel of 22.5 horsepower, adequate but not overly muscular for this heavy boat. It pushes her along at more than 5 knots in calm water at about 75 percent of full power, and it will take her up to hull speed of slightly more than 6.5 knots with the throttle wide open, at which stage it will consume about one gallon of fuel an hour. If you're happy to cruise along gently at 4 to 5 knots, as you might in the doldrums, your fuel consumption will shrink to about half a gallon an hour, greatly increasing your range under power and adding substantially, through diminished noise and vibration, to your quality of life. There's 25 gallons of fuel in the tank under the cockpit sole, enough if used wisely to take you 200 miles or more.

Owners replacing the original engine with the newer 27-hp Yanmar report that the extra 5 horsepower makes a difference when it comes to pushing the Nicholson 31 into strong headwinds and choppy seas.

Accommodations

The Nicholson 31 philosophy is so determinedly fixed on long-distance cruising that it seems almost whimsical to supply her with six full-sized berths. Boats of 31 feet with six berths are more usually weekenders or vacation boats, where people can go ashore or jump into the dinghy and ride around to get out of each others' way. Nobody in his or her right mind would want to cross an ocean cooped up with five other people in a Nicholson 31. And yet, to the consternation of any sane sailor, the berths are there: two up forward in a double V-berth, two settee berths in the main cabin, a pilot berth above and outside of the port settee berth, and a quarterberth whose head, peeking out from behind the chart table, accommodates the navigator's rear end while he or she attends to the charts.

> **In Short**
>
> **Nicholson 31**
>
> Designer: Camper & Nicholson, Ltd.
>
> LOA: 30 feet 7 inches
>
> LWL: 24 feet 2 inches
>
> Beam: 10 feet 3 inches
>
> Draft: 5 feet 0 inches
>
> Displacement: 14,750 pounds
>
> Sail area: 500 square feet
>
> Ballast: Encapsulated lead, 5,300 pounds
>
> Spars: Aluminum
>
> Auxiliary: Yanmar diesel 22.5 hp
>
> Designed as: Ocean cruiser

This is at least two berths too many, and the two most easily sacrificed would be one V-berth, which would make way for a more sensible workbench, and the pilot berth, which is mostly a vexing waste of space. The galley could benefit from more storage, and this would be a good place for it, along with a shelf for books and an additional locker or two. In most other respects, this boat is ideal for a cruising pair, even one with a couple of small kids.

There's a huge locker under the V-berth that will hold a year's supply of canned goods for two people.

Aft of the forward cabin is a thwartships head compartment, with a vacuum-operated Lavac toilet and a hanging locker to port, and a large washbasin and vanity to starboard. There's a pressure shower in there, but it's for masochists only. There's no hot water. The two sliding doors that separate the head/vanity compartment from the forecabin and the main saloon are heavy, and tend to stick in their slides when they haven't broken loose from their magnetic restraints at sea and tried to ram their way out through the hull. Not the cleverest of ideas. Most owners end up leaving them permanently open at sea, and sacrificing the modicum of privacy they offer, in exchange for the safety of the boat. Others have discarded the sliding doors and, with a little ingenious shaping, have fashioned a hinged marine ply door that shuts off the toilet only. It will also close off the main saloon, and hinge back against the main bulkhead inside the toilet compartment, right out of the way.

> ### In Comparison
> - Safety-at-sea factor: 3 (Rated against the 19 other boats in this book, with 1 being safest.)
> - Speed rating: Not fast to windward, but a good passagemaker when sailing free, capable of averaging 140 miles a day.
> - Ocean comfort level: Up to three adults in comfort; two adults and two kids in less comfort; four adults in relative discomfort.

Between the settee berths in the saloon is a very solid table, with a small, fiddled central section that stays permanently in place. It has leaves that hinge up on each side when required. It's a nice piece of furniture.

The galley, as usual, was designed by someone more interested in providing sleeping berths than decent cooking space. It's adequate, but only because most sailor's expectations are unusually low. Considering the importance of a galley, particularly on a liveaboard world cruiser, it's wonder the layout doesn't get more attention– and not just on the Nicholson. There are two stainless steel sinks, with fresh and salt water supplied, on a peninsula adjoining the aft end of the starboard settee, and outboard there is stowage for condiments, crockery, and cutlery. There is also a propane-fed two-burner stove and oven in gimbals. The icebox suffers from the usual north European malaise. In their culture, ice is a sinful luxury. It's equated with decadence and the most wicked form of high living. They really lust after it quite badly, but they know they shouldn't have it, so they compromise. They quell their consciences by making it difficult to get at. In the first place, the lid of the icebox is so small that you have to chop even a modest block of ice in two to get it in – which makes it melt twice as fast, of course. And, having got the ice in, there's precious little room for anything else. Even if you can squeeze a steak or two in there, or a pack of ice cream, you'll find no shelves to keep stuff off the ice. In the second place, the restricted amount of space over the icebox makes it inconvenient to stow or retrieve anything there. Deliberately inconvenient, presumably.

To compensate, there is a wonderful, sit-down navigation desk, big enough to take a full-sized chart folded only once. It faces forward, so the navigator doesn't get more confused than usual when plotting a course, and it hinges up to reveal stowage space for about 100 charts. Bulkheads and shelves forward of the table and to the side of it offer convenient sites for navigation instruments, books, radios, GPS, and the other paraphernalia that stirs a navigator's heart.

The Rig

The standard mast is a powerful aluminum extrusion from Proctor, untapered all the way up. The single pair of aluminum spreaders is shaped in an airfoil section. The basic sail area of this masthead sloop is a little short of 500 square feet, split almost evenly fore and aft of the keel-stepped mast.

The boom is equipped with easily worked slab reefing, and the mainsail comes with two rows of reef points sewn in. A third row is a good idea if you're not planning to carry a storm trysail. She has a single forestay and backstay of rugged proportions, and twin lower shrouds on each side. The mainsheet attaches well aft, clear of the cockpit, and foresail sheet winches are ready to hand. Everything is nicely set up for the singlehander.

Performance

You wouldn't expect this boat to be particularly closewinded or fast to weather– and she's neither. That is not to say, however, that she won't pluck herself off a lee shore with a lot of crashing and bashing when the need arises. She will plug away into heavy head seas far longer than most other boats of her size, using her considerable weight and momentum to punch her way through and gradually gain an offing.

But as soon as the wind is freed a bit, she comes into her own. She is beautifully balanced, requiring only the lightest touch on the tiller in any weather, and she tracks straight and true when running before the wind in heavy weather, rarely showing even the faintest inclination to broach to. With a reefed jib only, a self-steering vane gear will take her safely downwind in big following seas in 40 knots.

Under twin headsails, steered by a wind vane, she'll peel off 140 miles a day like clockwork with no help from her crew at all. She has the ability to heave to under a reefed mainsail only, riding the seas like a gull with her head under her wing, and in storm conditions too heavy even for heaving to, she lies ahull with reassuring steadiness, heeled over by the pressure of wind on her mast, and presenting her strongest area – the rounded sections of her hull – to the breaking waves.

Known Weaknesses

• She needs large headsails for decent light-weather performance.
• Price. Like all British-built boats, she's expensive in dollar terms.
• The miserable icebox.
• There's no provision below deck for a propane shut-off valve for the cooker.
Perhaps Europeans don't blow themselves up as frequently as Americans do, but for your own safety you should fit a valve that complies with the standards of the American Boat and Yacht Council.

Owner's Opinion

Art Stamey sails the Nicholson 31 *Desormais II* out of Everett, just north of Seattle, on Puget Sound. He bought her in 1986 from a Canadian who had already sailed her around Cape Horn. He had been wanting a Nicholson for some time. "Ferenc Mate's books sensitized me to the worth of Nicholson yachts. And the fact that they made Nelson's flagship, *Victory*, made it an acceptable yard for me."

In April, 1992, Stamey sailed her singlehanded to Raiatea, one of the islands of the Society group in the South Pacific. Later, he sailed her to Hawaii, a voyage of about 8,500 miles altogether. As a busy dentist, Stamey had little spare time, so he had a friend sail her back from Hawaii to Everett.

When Stamey left Neah Bay, in the Strait of Juan de Fuca, on his outbound leg, it was in the face of a storm warning. "I was well prepared," he said. "The storm was forecast for 48 hours hence and I thought *Well, let's get out to sea and see what she can do.* I was a good 100 miles offshore when it struck, and she was surprisingly comfortable.

"The outstanding feature of this boat is her ability to heave to with the tiller lashed to leeward slightly. She sits like a duck on the water in winds up to 50 knots under a third-reefed mainsail only."

Her best point of sail, he said, is a broad reach. "She handles beautifully then, carrying a full main and a working jib in winds of 25 knots with the Aries self-steering vane doing all the steering. It's a very seakindly point of sailing."

Desormais II carried a bit of weather helm, but not much. "On the whole she was nicely balanced."

Stamey's first action in rising wind was to reduce the roller-furling 110-percent headsail down to about 90 percent. Then, if the wind increased further, he'd take the first reef in mainsail; then a second reef in main. In even stronger winds, he'd furl the foresail completely and set a storm jib. Finally, in storm-force winds, he'd strike the jib and heave to under just the mainsail with three reefs – the equivalent of a storm trysail. He never felt apprehensive about the cockpit's being too big. "It has huge scuppers draining out through the transom. I never felt scared of a pooping."

He said the original Yanmar 22.5-hp diesel engine was perfectly adequate with a twin-bladed propeller.

His summing up: "She's a seakindly, dry boat, very well constructed. I have no complaints about the interior. It's not luxurious, but it's not Spartan either."

His advice for anyone planning to take a Nicholson 31 across an ocean:

• Check the mast inserts for the shroud terminals. They're stainless steel liners. His cracked, and he replaced them all.

• Bulwarks would afford a better foothold on the sidedecks in bad weather.

• Fit a boom gallows. "It's great for grabbing on at any time, and it's a very handy place to steady yourself against while you take sextant sights."

Conclusion

This is a boat you can trust in any weather far out to sea. She doesn't have the "traditional" looks of a round-the-worlder – neither bowsprit nor teak-laid decks – but she'll perform as well as any Colin Archer type, and in some situations much better. She has just the right amount of room for a cruising couple, and plenty of stowage space for their gear and provisions. She's docile, undemanding, and responsive to the helm – a delightful boat to sail on long passages.

A used Nicholson 31 will set you back anything between $30,000 and $50,000, depending on age and condition. You might have to be patient, because they are fairly scarce in the United States, and owners tend to hang on to them. But if you can't wait, there are usually plenty for sale in Britain. Why not buy one over there and sail her back?

Chapter Seventeen
Pacific Seacraft 25

She's at Home on Highway or Ocean

The Pacific Seacraft 25 is a dark horse. She's not built any longer, except perhaps to special order, and comparatively few people know her, yet she is remarkable in this respect: She is a trailerable sailboat fully fit to take on the ocean.

A *Cruising World* article once described this cocky little 25-footer her as "the perfect trailerable offshore family cruiser offering seaworthiness, ease of handling, speed, comfort, and years of safe low-maintenance voyaging."

The magazine went on to say that "her traditional double-ended hull is patterned after the famous No Man's Land boats of the 19th century, which were able to carry heavy loads and sail swiftly and safely in all types of weather."

Well, perhaps the author of that glowing account was wearing rose-colored spectacles that day. Perfect she is not, neither is she swift. But one has to admit that the hyperbole this rugged cruiser generates among her admirers is very infectious. And if she's not perfect it hardly matters because she exudes that magical combination of allure and seduction that makes perfection quite unnecessary.

Although she's trailerable, she's not the sort of weekend trailer-sailer you take to the lake for an afternoon's relaxation. This boat weighs more than 2 tons and draws more than 3 feet, so it would take time and planning to launch her and retrieve her. On the other hand, you can haul her out, take her home, and leave her in your driveway for the winter. You can see her every day then, and drag the neighbors in to admire her. Like many fine cruising yachts, she shows her workboat heritage in simple, no-nonsense lines. No wasteful overhangs for her, just the longest possible waterline for cargo-carrying capacity. No chrome, no tinsel, no smoke and mirrors, just good solid oak, teak, and bronze. She has the mien of a voyager about her, a restless, purposeful appearance. She wants to go to sea.

Basic Design

The Pacific Seacraft Corporation's 25-footer looks as much like a ship's lifeboat as a fishing vessel. She's apple-cheeked and buoyant up forward, and her topsides are probably a little higher than those of a fishing boat but do not detract from her handsome looks. Her rudder hangs on a sharply raked sternpost, like a Folkboat's, and it is a measure of this boat's ruggedness that the rudder's oak cheeks are fastened in place by no fewer than 11 bolts.

The hull is hand-laminated with a high glass-to-resin ratio for extra strength, and the topsides are scored lengthwise to resemble wooden carvel planking. The decks and cabintop are balsa cored for lightness and strength.

The forward face of the cabin trunk is high, boxy and unrelievedly white. It glares at you with a baleful blank stare, daring you to spray graffiti on it. It's probably the least attractive part of this boat but its looks could be improved considerably with the clever use of paint or a strip or two of teak.

There is a gunwale of sorts: It's a couple of inches high at the bow, and gradually fades out to nothing at the cockpit. It's topped with a teak caprail almost wide enough to skateboard on. Her keel is a modified traditional shape, a full-length keel cut away at the forefoot and also (because of the rake of the sternpost) at the heel. Nevertheless, a long straight section remains, flat on the bottom for a good length, so that she will take the ground without falling flat on her face.

The cabintop, although rather high, is not unduly obtrusive, except at its forward edge, as we have mentioned already, and the sidedecks are reasonably wide – getting wider, in fact, as you move forward. The sliding cover over the companionway hatch runs in deep grooves, but lacks a seahood, or turtle, to prevent heavy spray driving underneath it and entering the cabin.

In Short

Pacific Seacraft 25

Designer: Pacific Seacraft Corporation, 1979

LOA: 26 feet 3 inches

LOD: 24 feet 6 inches

LWL: 21 feet 0 inches

Beam: 8 feet 0 inches

Draft: 3 feet 3 inches

Displacement: 4,750 pounds

Sail area: 250 square feet

Ballast: 1,750 pounds

Spars: Aluminum

Auxiliary:
Yanmar 8-hp diesel

Designed as: Trailerable pocket offshore cruiser

The self-draining cockpit is snug and solid. It has a very pleasing feeling of security; and here, as everywhere else on this boat, the metal fittings are substantial hunks of stainless steel or bronze. It has two drains at the forward edge – it could probably do with two more for serious sea work – but it has no bridgedeck, only a 9-inch sill to stop water flooding below. This means you'd need to keep one or two companionway washboards in place at sea and make sure they were fixed in place with barrel bolts or some such arrangement. The whole of the cockpit floor is one big hatch cover with downturned flanges that fit over a sill with upturned edges. If you undo 25 fat screws you can lift it out and gain splendid access to the engine and the stuffing box, but it is a large area to seal satisfactorily, and if it isn't watertight it will admit large portions of the ocean when a wave fills the cockpit. The standard engine is an 8-horsepower Yanmar diesel that fits into the space under the cockpit as a finger fits in a glove. Access from the cabin is minimal; if you remove the companionway step you can peer at the engine hopefully and wipe its little face, but that's about all. If you're desperate enough, you can undo four screws and remove a panel adjacent to the starboard quarterberth. Then you can get to the engine, or at least to one side of it, either by leaning around the corner awkwardly or by lying full-length on your side in the quarterberth.

Accommodations

It's surprising, given the height of the cabintop, that there isn't more headroom down

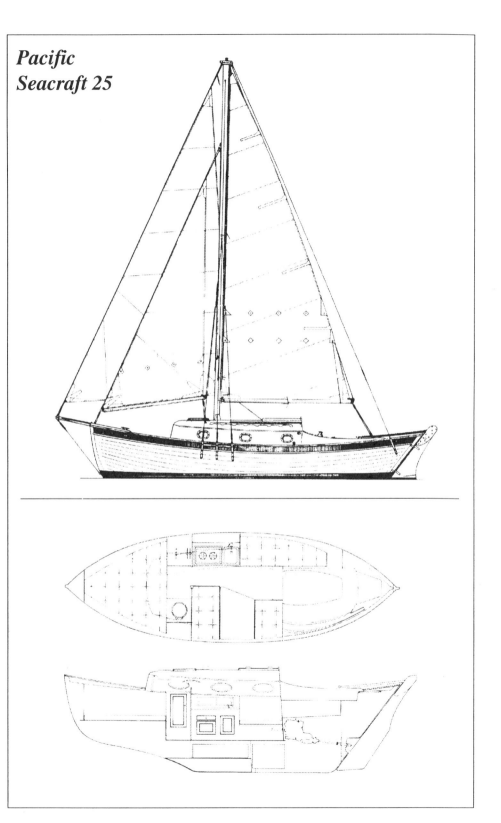

Pacific Seacraft 25

below, but it's just as well that the impulse to make the cabintop even taller was resisted, for that would surely have turned her into a duckling so ugly not even her mother could have loved her. As it is, the headroom is about 5 feet, which is of no consequence when you're at sea, and which you can endure with good grace in port if you are a person of even temper and likeable nature. There are no overhead beams to hit your head on – it's covered with a zippered headliner.

Right up forward in the fo'c's'le there's a pretty teak door you should open with caution. It allows access to the chain locker, and if the chain is piled up high it will spill out all over you as soon as you slide back the barrel bolt.

Aft of the door is a V-berth in the form of an isosceles triangle. If you and your partner have sharply tapered hips, legs, and feet, it will fit you fine. Otherwise it's best left to kids. The hull up here is covered with a glued-on fabric that the kids will probably pull off. There is a deep storage locker under the V-berth.

Also in the forecabin are a head, to port, and a half-length hanging cupboard with a shelf on top, to starboard. A curtain on a swinging arm separates the forecabin from the main saloon. Probably the most prominent feature of the saloon is the portside dinette, an arrangement of two thwartship seats with a raised table in between. The forward seat accommodates two people side by side, the aft seat just one. The outer edge of the table is tapered to fit neatly between them. The table can be lowered to turn the seats into a double berth, which, although it, too, is tapered, offers more foot room than does the V-berth. To starboard, convenient to the double seat, is a galley of generous size with a two-burner alcohol stove, a sink, and neat teak racks for dishes, mugs, and cutlery. There is stowage for provisions beneath the stove and in an enormous louvered locker under the double seat.

Aft of the galley is a snug quarterberth, bringing the total number of berths to five. That's three too many for a dedicated cruising boat of this size, but fine for family vacation cruising or short coastal hops.

The joinerwork is first-class, as is only to be expected from this manufacturer, and the fittings substantial. Six solid bronze portlights, all opening, and an overhead hatch bring light and plenty of ventilation to both cabins. The cabin sole is oak parquet on a plywood backing.

The Rig

The Pacific Seacraft 25 is a masthead cutter or sloop with a sail area of 250 square feet. Her bowsprit is quite short, and the staysail stay comes down to the stemhead, so there is not a lot of breathing room for the jib in the cutter version. Nevertheless, she badly needs the extra area of a large genoa jib to keep her moving in light weather, and it must breathe as best it can.

The spars are painted aluminum and the mainsail is equipped with slab reefing. The mast, which has a single spreader and fore-and-aft lower shrouds, is stepped on deck in a tabernacle that allows the spar to be dropped and raised quickly. A substantial wooden compression post attached to a half bulkhead transfers the downward thrust of the rig to the keel. The main boom is fairly short, so no boomkin is needed, just a split backstay, bowsed down to the quarters, to give the tiller swinging room. The shroud chainplates are placed on the outside of the hull and secured by four bolts each. The mainsheet runs through quarter blocks on either side of the tiller and is easily accessible at the helm. Tracks for sliding foresail sheet blocks are screwed to the caprail either side of the cockpit.

Performance

The fact that the PS 25 has earned a racing handicap rating must prove something, even if her PHRF number is 312, but no tactful person mentions speed and PS 25 in the same breath. Luckily, there are other facets to performance, and it is in these that she shines. Her buoyant ends will keep her dry, and her long keel will make her track straight and true. She'll heave to well, and run before big seas in safety with just a windvane steering her. Her little Yanmar produces more than 3 horsepower per ton of displacement, so she will reach her hull speed of 6 knots with ease in calm weather although she might struggle just a little against a strong wind and heavy seas. It is important to fit the correct propeller – one that will allow the engine to reach top revolutions (and therefore produce most power) in heavy going. Yes, the PS 25 performs well, no doubt about. She's just not known for speed.

Known Weaknesses

• Check the cockpit floor for leaks.
• Check the main sliding hatch cover for leaks from driving spray, and fit a top cover if necessary.
• Install fittings that allow the two lower dropboards to be securely fastened in place at sea.

Owner's Opinion

Steve Way, of Tacoma, Washington, owned a Pacific Seacraft 25 for nearly two years. He sailed her many hundreds of miles all over Puget Sound and the Canadian Gulf Islands, and completed two circumnavigations of Vancouver Island in her.

"She was a great little boat," he said. "She was fun to sail. I sailed with kids, and they could handle her easily. I would take a PS 25 across an ocean without hesitation."

There's weight behind those words. Between 1993 and 1997, Way circumnavigated the world in a boat not much bigger than the PS 25. She was a Laurent Giles-designed bilge-keeler, a Westerly 26 named *Lookfar*.

His PS 25 was rigged as a sloop, and had no bowsprit. "She was initially tender," he recalls, "but after heeling a little, she stiffened up. She wasn't a fast boat, but she went well on a reach." He carried a cruising spinnaker and found it an asset in light weather.

She behaved impeccably in heavy weather during one of Way's cruises around rugged Vancouver Island.

In Comparison

• Safety-at-sea factor: 18 (Rated against the 19 other boats in this book, with 1 being safest.)

• Speed rating: With a PHRF rating of 312, speed is not this boat's best asset. By way of comparison, another well-known 25-footer, the International Folkboat, rates 234, which means she covers a distance of one nautical mile 78 seconds faster than the PS 25, on average, around a race course.

• Ocean comfort level: One or two adults.

"We were on the west coast, which is wide open to the North Pacific, and it started to blow out of the north. The swells built up, too, and eventually we were running under storm jib only. She handled the swells beautifully, with no tendency to broach. I don't know what the windspeed was, but a large powerboat came into port after us and reported winds of 45 knots."

What about the lack of headroom? "It was a non-factor. It never bothered me."

Way has owned several boats since then, but he still recalls that his PS 25 was well finished and very strong. "She also had a sweet little single-cylinder Yanmar engine that you could start by hand. It gave her full hull speed."

The one piece of advice he has for anyone intending to go to sea in a PS 25 is this: "Keep the two lower dropboards in place all the time. Secure them well."

Conclusion

You should be able to buy a used PS 25 for between $15,000 and $20,000 depending on her condition and upgrades. That makes her very reasonably priced for an ocean-going boat. Her tough construction makes her cheap to maintain, and the fact that you can pull her out on a trailer any time you want means you'll save on boatyard bills. If you're short of time, the trailer will also enable you to spend sailing vacations in exotic spots you'd never have time to reach ordinarily.

The PS 25 is a sweet-natured little boat and a good singlehander. It's almost certain she'd still be in production if she had the standing headroom that modern sailors have become used to. Meanwhile, if you don't mind doing the PS 25 crouch now and then, she's a bargain waiting to be snapped up.

Chapter Eighteen
Pearson Triton 28

A Worthy Son of Neptune

They're everywhere. More than 700 Carl Alberg-designed Tritons were built between 1959 and 1967 by Pearson Yachts in Rhode Island and Aeromarine Plastics in California, and most of them are still floating. Many have undertaken serious voyages, for this skinny Scandinavian was designed to be at home on blue water.

Alberg, who is well represented in this book, was of Swedish descent himself, of course, and much influenced by European standards of seaworthiness as they had evolved in working boats over the centuries. There's a little of the Viking longboat in the Triton, and more than a little of the Folkboat.

Besides her distinguished designer, the Triton has her own niche in the maritime hall of fame. She was one of the first boats in the United States to be built of fiberglass, a technique so different from traditional wooden boatbuilding methods that it stood the whole industry on its head.

At 28 feet overall, with a displacement of about 8,000 pounds, the Triton is on the verge of being a splendid cruising boat for two people. She teeters on the verge only because of her small interior (inevitable in a boat so skinny and short on the waterline) not for any want of seaworthiness. Even the small interior wouldn't matter quite so much if a bit more of it were devoted to the galley.

She does have low freeboard, it must be admitted, so she isn't as dry on deck as are some of her more modern sisters when the wind is on the nose, but she makes up for it in looks. Those of us who studied the Triton's lines on paper for years before we saw a real, live one, were belatedly surprised by her good looks. Her delicate stern and gentle sheer had always seemed to be badly marred by that tall, slabsided doghouse protruding skyward at the aft end of the cabintop. But, upon closer acquaintance, that doghouse wasn't nearly as repulsive in reality as it had been on paper, and if you stationed yourself off to one quarter while she waltzed away from you, flirting and showing her gorgeous transom, your gaze never reached the doghouse anyway.

But we must not get fixated on looks, important as they are. The two major assets of the Triton are these:

• Even after all these years, most Tritons are capable of going to sea. Many do. At least one has circumnavigated. Some will need to be upgraded, and those that haven't been properly maintained will need a thorough refit, but basically they are sturdy boats of inherently seaworthy design that will look after you in bad weather.

• They're cheap. You'll find bargain basement Tritons going for $10,000 or less and nicely fitted-out Tritons for $15,000.

Basic Design

Like many boats of her era, the Triton's design was influenced indirectly by the Cruising Club of America (CCA) rule. Quite coincidentally, this rule fit well with Alberg's basic design philosophy. He was a proponent of the type: large mainsail, small foresail, low freeboard, and moderately long overhangs fore and aft. To this he added a traditional full keel, except that he cut it away up forward and sloped it inward from the stern, so that it appeared to be starting the metamorphosis toward a fin keel. Most noticeably, Alberg made her beam quite narrow so she would slip through the water more easily. In this respect, he sacrificed accommodations for performance; but in those days it didn't matter because almost all boats followed the same pattern. It wasn't until a decade later that the "normal" boat began to be wide and shallow, rather than deep and narrow – and the sacrifice these latter boats made for the interior space they gained was seaworthiness. Within reasonable limits, narrow and deep is safer at sea than shallow and wide, although if you're not planning to cross an ocean, as most production-boat owners are not, you can afford to sacrifice a certain amount of safety because you're never far from help and shelter.

The hull of the Triton is solid fiberglass, varying from about 3/8 inch at the sheerline to about 3/4 inch in the keel area. The decks are also fiberglass, cored with end-grain balsa. Early boats had external ballast keels and keel bolts, but a little over halfway through the production run a change was made to a cast-lead keel encapsulated in the fiberglass hull. The ballast amounts to about 40 percent of total displacement and gives her a wide range of stability. Although the Triton has reasonably hard bilges, which spells good form stability, her narrow beam causes her to heel over 10 or 15 degrees before the keel really starts to show who's in charge.

Her foredeck is wide and reasonably clear of obstructions, and while it would be wonderful if a fairy could wave her magic wand and make the sidedecks wider, it isn't going to happen except in your dreams. About all you can say of them is that they're manageable. You might also wish that if the fairy could spare a second wave of her wand, something aesthetic would happen to the doghouse, that upward step in the coachroof. It's more likely, however, that her wand would short out, or blow a transistor, when faced with a task of such magnitude.

The cockpit is more than 6 feet long, but it has a bridgedeck to keep water out of the accommodations and it is narrow enough that it ships no water when the boat is laid flat on her beam ends. In any case, owners report that it doesn't hold enough water, even after a pooping, to threaten the safety of the boat.

The original rudders were wooden, made of mahogany, and while they have many advantages, they do tend to deteriorate over lifetimes as long as those the Tritons appear to be enjoying. You can have a new rudder made of fiberglass, but you can also laminate a new one from marine plywood if you have the time and inclination.

In Short
Pearson Triton 28
Designer: Carl Alberg (1959)
LOA: 28 feet 6 inches
LWL: 20 feet 6 inches
Beam: 8 feet 3 inches
Draft: 4 feet 0 inches
Displacement: 8,000 pounds
Sail area: 362 square feet
Ballast: Lead, 3,019 pounds
Spars: Aluminum
Auxiliary: 30-hp Universal Atomic 4 gasoline
Designed as: Coastal/ocean cruiser

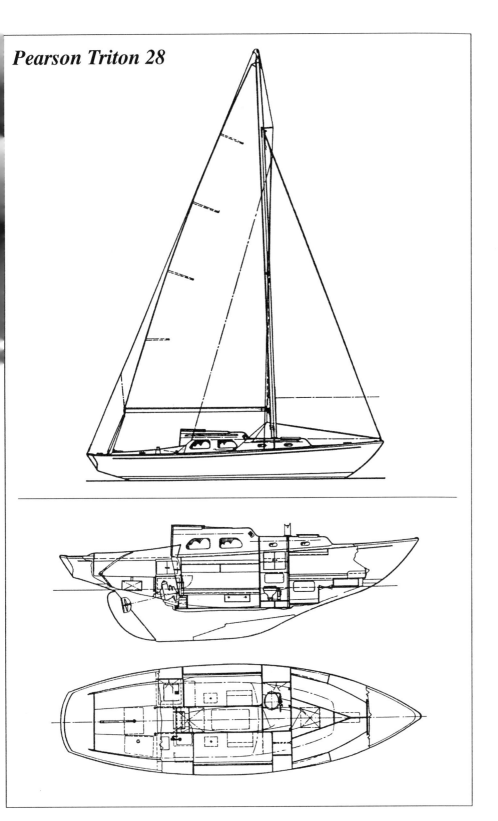

Pearson Triton 28

The original engine was the venerable Atomic 4, a 30-hp, four-cylinder gasoline engine designed from the very start for marine use by the Universal company. By today's standards, it's quite crude – but that it gives it certain advantages denied to modern diesels. If you have even the most rudimentary knowledge of how an internal combustion engine works, you can usually coax an Atomic 4 into life. It will absorb an extraordinary amount of abuse and still get you home on two cylinders. You can attack it with crude wrenches that would cause thousands of dollars'-worth of damage to a finely engineered diesel, and take pieces away to your local blacksmith for repair. Parts are still available, as are reconditioned engines and books on repair and maintenance. *Good Old Boat* magazine (www.goodoldboat.com) has published an extensive series of articles about the Atomic 4. Thirty horsepower is far more than the Triton needs, of course, but it means you'll achieve hull speed with half the noise and a quarter the vibration of a comparable diesel.

Accommodations

For a boat only 20 feet long on the waterline, the Triton has a reasonable, if not generous, amount of room below, thanks largely to the high cabintop. You'll find more than 6 feet of headroom beneath the doghouse roof in the main cabin, and a little less as you move forward.

The usual V-berths reside in the fo'c's'le, but they're not really usable at sea, and in port they're probably better left to the kids. Aft of the V-berths there's a separate but rather small head compartment (designated on Pearson's plans as a rather posher-sounding "toilet room") with a linen locker; and opposite, to starboard, a capacious hanging locker and shelf.

The settee berths in the main cabin are 6 feet 3 inches long and awkwardly wide – too wide for sitting without something to support your back, too narrow for a double berth. In the vertical step between the cabintop and the doghouse, Pearson built in two opening portholes. These not only greatly help ventilation below but offer you the chance, when you're anchored in a heavy blow, to stand on tip-toe down below in the comfort of your own cabin and see the other boats dragging down onto you.

Aft of the settees we stumble across the Triton's disaster area, the galley. Although the Swedes are not renowned for their haut cuisine, it's hard to believe that Alberg so hated food that he refused to leave space for a permanent cooker. No doubt it was the usual pressure from Pearson's sales staff for the greatest possible number of beds that forced the decision upon him. In any case, most Triton owners have had to fend for themselves. Most use portable stoves, which is not a solution for a deepsea voyager. Others have bolted a gimbaled, single-burner to a bulkhead. That works, but it isn't exactly clever or efficient. It's a sad thing, but the galley of the Triton will never be recognized as Alberg's magnum opus.

The Rig

Most Tritons are Bermudian sloops, but a yawl rig was available and a few were built. Some sloops – in fact all the early ones – were fractionally rigged, with the forestay joining the mast about three-quarters of the way up, where the mast was beefed up with jumper struts. Later, Pearson's offered a masthead rig with a shorter mast.

The earliest Tritons, the first 100 or so, had only single lower shrouds, but after complaints that they were inadequate, Pearson's changed the rig to double lowers. The sail area of the fractional sloop is 371 square feet, with 231 square feet of that in the mainsail and 140 square feet in the working jib.

The aluminum mast is stepped on deck and therefore prone to the usual problem of crushing the cabin beam supporting it. The narrowness of the gangway below makes it difficult to slide past a keel-stepped mast but if you're thinking of buying a Triton for long-distance voyaging, you might want to consider installing a solid compression post from directly beneath the mast step to the ballast keel, even if you have to suck in your tummy to get past it. It's the quickest, easiest, and strongest solution to a vexing problem.

The boom is 14 feet long and covers most of the cockpit, so the anchor point for the mainsheet is conveniently far aft, on the little lazarette deck, where the sheet is out of everybody's way.

Performance

As the Triton heels, her long overhangs dip into the water and effectively lengthen her waterline. As the maximum speed of a displacement boat is directly related to her waterline length, the Triton should be capable of faster maximum speeds when she's well heeled over than when she's upright. That is the theory, anyway, and it is frequently propounded by shallow thinkers. Deeper thought will reveal the fact that, in practice, she'll rarely reach hull speed under sail while heeled far over (except occasionally on a broad reach, when everybody else is going fast, too) and her performance at less than full speed might even *suffer* from heeling because she's immersing more hull area and creating more drag. No matter. Suffice it to say that the Triton is a reasonably fast boat if she has good sails and you sail her well. Her performance to windward is probably better than that of most cruisers, and as for the rest of them, it simply isn't fair to compare her with racers or modern coastal cruisers of similar size. They're faster, but they pay for it in other ways. Her PHRF rating, for what it's worth, is about 246.

She seems to be a little tender at first, which, if you've been plowing through this book vessel by vessel, you will now recognize as the sign of a comfortable sea-boat. She heels over quite easily to 10 degrees or a little more, after which gravity wakes up the sleeping ballast keel and puts it to work. She becomes increasingly more difficult to tip over, and owners report that it's not easy to submerge the toerail.

She does carry weather helm as the wind pipes up, however, and your first move to cure it is to reef the mainsail. If you have to go down to a working jib or a storm jib, you will need a deep double reef in the mainsail to keep her balanced.

Apart from that slight weather helm, she appears to have no vices, and steering control remains good because she doesn't lift her rudder out of the water when she's heeled excessively, like some IOR racers we know – and

In Comparison

- Safety-at-sea factor: 12 (Rated against the 19 other boats in this book, with 1 being safest.)
- Speed rating: Average PHRF rating of 246 makes her sound slower than she really is, but she's not a flyer.
- Ocean comfort level: One or two adults in comfort, plus two kids at a squeeze.

their derivative coastal cruisers. Under power, with the Atomic 4 slaving away in the bilge, she will easily reach her top speed of 6 knots under almost any conditions. With more than 8 horsepower per ton of displacement, the Atomic 4 provides twice the power she needs.

Known Weaknesses

• Check the decks and cabintop decks for delamination caused by a balsa core saturated with water. Delaminated areas sound dull and hollow, or flex excessively, when you tap them with the handle of a screwdriver or jump on them.

• If you have an early model with an external ballast keel, check the keel bolts for corrosion.

• Mast compression: Look for signs of cracking, bending, movement, or crushing in the mast-support beam and the timbers that transfer the thrust to the main bulkhead. If the beam has failed, you'll either have to replace it – a major repair – or ignore it and fit a new compression post, as suggested above under the heading The Rig.

• Check the whole rig. There have been reported failures of tangs.

• Inspect the wooden rudder for rot or woodworm.

Owner's Opinion

Probably the most famous owner of a Pearson Triton is Dan Spurr, Editor of *Practical Sailor* and a former senior editor on the staff of *Cruising World* magazine.

Spurr lived aboard his Triton, *Adriana*, and put up with her little faults for five years. Then he launched on a program that involved major changes to her interior.

If you own a Triton and want to make similar changes you are lucky. Spurr gives detailed instructions and descriptions of all the improvements he made to *Adriana* in his book *Upgrading the Cruising Sailboat*, (International Marine Publishers, 1991), which is lavishly illustrated by the well-known marine artist Bruce Bingham, designer of the Flicka 20. With a few basic tools and a few basic skills, you can convert the V-berth to a comfortable double bed, install a new engine, improve the much-maligned galley, and make all kinds of beneficial changes to your Triton. Spurr also cruised many hundreds of miles in *Adriana*, in the USA and the Bahamas, so he knows the boat as well as anybody. If you're considering taking a Triton for a ride over the horizon, *Upgrading the Cruising Sailboat* (otherwise known as *Spurr's Boatbook*) is not just a good idea; it's *compulsory* reading.

Conclusion

The last Triton was built in 1967, so they're all getting a bit long in the tooth. Nevertheless, if you buy one that has been reasonably well maintained, you'll have a boat that's still capable of crossing oceans.

Practical Sailor magazine calls the Triton "the smallest, most affordable offshore boat you can buy. At least one has circumnavigated – Jim Baldwin in *Atom* – and we know of many others that have made safe transoceanic passages."

Carl Alberg probably never dreamed his creation would one day earn such a flattering epithet.

Chapter Nineteen
Southern Cross 31

She Gives You That Burning Yearning

If you've ever stood on a dock alongside a Southern Cross 31 you'll know the meaning of the word yearning. It's that deep and anxious longing or desire you feel as you run your eyes over her deck and rigging.

The desire hits you on two levels. The first longing is for the boat herself, this pretty little creature with the delicate sheerline and the cheeky little bowsprit. The second, almost simultaneous longing is for the exotic places she can take you to, places where the constellation after which she's named hangs high in the southern sky. Suddenly your nostrils tingle with the hot spicy scent of a tropical island. And what's that on deck just forward of the cockpit? Could it be white coral sand from somebody's bare feet? Ah yes, this is truly a boat to yearn over, a beautiful boat just longing to visit the earth's beautiful places.

Colin Archer, the famous Scotsman who lived in Norway and produced designs of sail-powered sea-rescue boats, would have approved of the Southern Cross 31. She has much the same sort of underwater body as Archer's much revered designs, a full keel with a long flat section at the bottom, and not much of a cutaway forward. She also has an outboard rudder and the famous pointed stern that was said to make the Colin Archers so seaworthy in heavy following seas.

From 1975 to 1987, more than 130 fiberglass SC 31s were built by the C. E. Ryder corporation in Newport, Rhode Island, and about half of them were sold as uncompleted hulls to do-it-yourselfers. For this reason, although they all look similar on deck, you never know what you'll find below on this boat. The factory-finished boats have a standard interior layout, but home-builders always have their own ideas and they're inevitably better than the designer's ideas – or so the meddlers think. Mostly, in fact, they're not, but there may be a few that will surprise you. The price of a used SC 31 varies according to the design and finish of her interior, too. You might find an early one being offered for somewhere around $35,000 to $40,000; later models finished professionally will cost proportionately more. But if you can afford it, it's a relatively cheap ride to paradise.

Basic Design

Thomas Gillmer, the designer of the Southern Cross 31, is much admired for seaworthy cruisers constructed in a robust traditional manner. His credentials are impressive. He was professor of Naval Architecture at the U.S. Naval Academy in Annapolis, and headed the design department.

The SC 31, interestingly enough, is actually a close cousin of another famous boat that came off his drawing board – the Seawind, built by Allied, which was the first sailboat built of fiberglass to circumnavigate the world. The Seawind was the forerunner of the Seawind II, another of the ocean-proven designs described in this book. The SC 31 is really a Seawind with the aft end changed from a transom stern to a double-ender and a few other alterations. She has a little more beam, a little more internal volume, and her displacement has gone up half a ton.

One of this boat's claims to fame is that her hull is cored with Airex foam. That makes her more buoyant in case of a bad leak, and it also insulates the interior against cold and noise. The condensation so often found inside fiberglass hulls in cold waters is almost non-existent in this boat, and the thudding of waves against the topsides is far more muted than it is in solid fiberglass boats.

No material is perfect, however, and some critics express concern about the strength of a cored hull – not its mechanical strength or rigidity, which is probably far greater than that of a solid fiberglass layup, but its ability to resist punctures. The critics maintain that two thin skins of brittle fiberglass with a thick soft core in the middle are not as safe as one thick skin of fiberglass. Their worries stem from the fact that the outer skin is more easily penetrated by a sharp object in the water, a deadhead hit at speed, or a rock pinnacle that the boat has run up on. It's rather like a balloon that, blown up too tightly, can be exploded with the slightest prick of a pin. On the SC 31, it's a question of impact resistance, of course, and some people believe the SC 31 is lacking in this respect, at least in theory. Those of us who have no way of discovering whether this is a real problem or merely a hypothesis propounded by nautical naysayers console ourselves with the thought that even if the outside skin is punctured, there is another skin inside, plus that extra thickness of plastic foam. We can hardly believe it would be more dangerous than a single solid skin cracked right through.

Because foam is reputed to be adversely affected by the sun's heat, the fiberglass decks and cabin roof are cored with edge-grain balsa, which is more forgiving. It's also standard practice in most production boats. In areas of stress, or where fittings are likely to be bolted right through the deck, solid plywood is substituted for balsa.

The boat's underwater profile, as we've already seen, is old-fashioned, well tested, and therefore greatly comforting to conservative cruisers. The outboard rudder is efficient and easy to get to if anything goes wrong.

It's the modern fashion to cut away more of the keel's forefoot than Gillmer did on the SC 31, and this helps in two ways: firstly, it reduces the surface area of the underwater hull, and therefore the resistance it produces. Secondly, it makes the hull more maneuverable, at very slight cost to its ability to keep tracking in a straight line. It also, incidentally, moves the center of lateral resistance aft, which helps resist a boat's tendency to gripe, or bore into the wind – the phenomenon known to practical sailors as weather helm.

But the oldtimers gave their boats deep forefeet for good reasons. That amount of grip on the water, so far forward, helps a boat heave to quietly and mind her own business when you leave her under reefed sails with the helm lashed to leeward slightly, and the old working boats from which this design sprang had to endure many hours of

Southern Cross 31

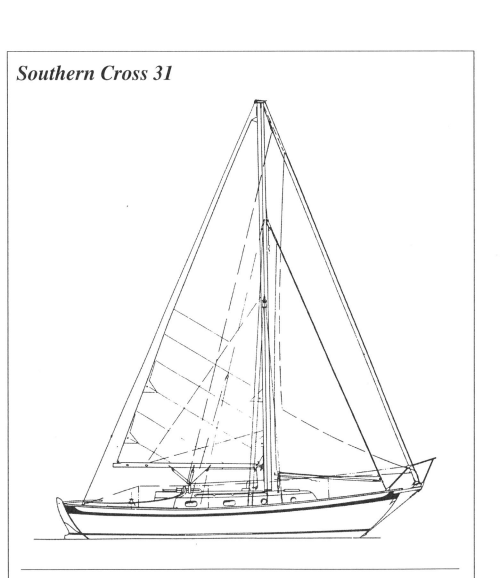

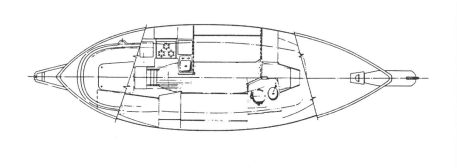

gales at sea with their heads tucked under their wings in this fashion. The downside of a deep forefoot is that a boat running with too much canvas in a capful of wind and large swells may tend to trip over her keel and broach to. But with reasonable caution and ordinary care, this situation should never arise; and in any case, we're talking here of mere degrees of risk. There is no implication here that a boat with a deep forefoot is inherently unseaworthy. An overcanvased fin keeler is far more likely to broach to under those conditions than is any boat with a traditional keel. All boats have strong points and weak points; the best sailors know which is which, and act accordingly.

The SC 31's coachroof is quite low and streamlined. Her topsides are low, too, so she presents little top hamper to the wind. Her sidedecks are reasonably wide for easy movement fore and aft, and she has bulwarks to delight the hearts of those of us who habitually drop the pin of every shackle we open and live in fear of the "ping-splash" that signifies its loss forever. The bulwarks are also very comforting when you have to walk along a leeward sidedeck that's under water, of course.

In Short

Southern Cross 31

Designer: Tom Gillmer (1976)
LOA: 31 feet 0 inches
LWL: 25 feet 0 inches
Beam: 9 feet 6 inches
Draft: 4 feet 7 inches
Displacement: 13,600 pounds
Sail area: 447 square feet
Ballast: Encapsulated lead, 4,400 pounds
Spars: Aluminum
Auxiliary: 22-hp diesel
Designed as: Conservative bluewater cruiser

The cockpit is small: that is to say it's the right size for sea work. It won't accommodate the whole family, complete with grandparents and kids, for Thanksgiving dinner, but it does provide a safe haven for a lonely watchkeeper or two in the wee hours of the morning. It also has that most desirable feature in an ocean-going boat, a nice strong bridgedeck.

The weighted keel is a lead casting encapsulated within the hull. It weighs about 4,400 pounds, which is about 32 percent of the boat's displacement, just about the right amount to give her an easy motion at sea.

Given the high number of home-finished boats, the auxiliary engine could be almost anything, but most of them will have a 22-hp diesel squeezed under the companionway steps. That's plenty for a 6-tonner, and should give her a range of 250 miles or more, thanks to the 34-gallon fuel tank.

Accommodations

For a boat displacing more than 6 tons, there is not a lot of room down below on the SC 31, but she will accommodate two adults, maybe three, in reasonable comfort on long passages, and more for shorter coastal trips. The forward cabin has the usual V-berth arrangement, which is awkward to scramble into and out of at the best of times. At sea, it's mostly unusable and becomes ad hoc storage for everything from the deflated rubber dinghy to the spare stormsail. It would be far more useful on a long-distance cruising yacht to convert this cabin into a workshop with a bench and generous storage areas, but on production yachts it's almost always crammed with sleeping places because a plenitude of berths is what the builder's sales department wants.

Aft of the fo'c's'le there's a head compartment to starboard and hanging space opposite. The main saloon is very straightforward: two settee berths, with a galley aft to port, and a chart table aft to starboard. A quarterberth was an option, but it meant a foldaway chart table instead of a fixed one, which a proper cruiser really needs quite badly. Nice as it is, the quarterberth won't be missed at sea if the number of crewmembers is kept down to one or two.

The galley, it must be admitted, is small and inadequate – but then, on a 31-footer it *usually* is, and the SC 31's galley is no smaller nor more inadequate than any other in its class. Yacht designers all seem to chant the same mantra in this connection: Seagoing cooks must suffer. And they do. Over the years of production, the galley did receive a little more attention, however, and the single sink became two sinks in a projecting peninsula, presumably to enable the cook to do twice the amount of washing up, or to finish the normal amount in half the time.

The standard of finish supplied by the Ryder corporation was commendably high. For example, there are eight ports in the coachroof sides, and they all can be opened. And if that's not enough in the way of ventilation, there are also two large opening hatches overhead.

The Rig

Tom Gillmer gave the SC 31 a modern masthead cutter rig, with a jib set from a short bowsprit and a staysail set from the stemhead. The total working sail area is just under 450 square feet, so the rig is easy for one person to handle.

This is yet another boat with an aluminum, deck-stepped mast, but it does at least have a wooden compression post to transfer the thrust directly to the keel. One wonders why so many designers shy away from keel-stepped masts, especially on pure cruisers, which are not so likely to be hauled and have the stick removed every winter. Mast partners add valuable strength and stiffness to a keel-stepped mast.

The original design featured a club on the foot of the staysail, but some owners will probably have discarded it in favor of a loose-footed sail because the cutter rig is already cluttered on a boat of this size. Besides, you really need a self-tending staysail only when you're contemplating frequent tacking, and that's something a deepsea cruiser shouldn't have to do.

Performance

While the SC 31 is no round-the-buoys racer, her long waterline helps her maintain respectable average speeds on long passages. Her modest draft of 4 feet 7 inches, combined with a low-aspect-ratio keel, means she's not going to pass any fin-keeled racer/cruisers on the beat, but she's capable of showing them a thing or two on a close reach in choppy head seas and, of course, she really comes into her own on beam and broad reaches. Some critics bent on gainsaying Professor Gillmer wonder whether the SC 31 is ballasted enough. Her design displacement is 13,600 pounds, of which about 32 percent (4,400 pounds) is a lead casting in the keel cavity. In the good professor's defense, it can be said that this was regarded as a perfectly acceptable ratio for working boats of this type, which carried their engines, fuel, water, and sometimes internal trimming ballast, low down in the hull. In those days, too, perhaps people showed more common sense about stowing heavy gear, books, and provisions as low as possible in the boat, and about keeping all these things place so they wouldn't shift during a rollover.

Known Weaknesses

• Although balsa-cored decks are standard among production boats, many suffer over the years from water intrusion, which leads to delamination and great loss of strength. If you're buying an old SC 31 check her decks and cabin top for hollow sounds and flexing.

• Check the outer skin of the hull carefully for punctures or cracks. Water won't necessarily penetrate the inner skin, or even spread through the plastic foam core, so this kind of damage is easy to overlook.

• Most factory-finished boats were supplied with alcohol stoves. They're not the best choice for ocean cruisers, who mostly prefer propane, kerosene, or even diesel cookers.

Owner's Opinion

Bob and Judy Boudrot sail their 1980 factory-finished Southern Cross 31, *Second Wind*, out of Manchester-by-the-Sea, Mass. Bob, Vice-Commodore of the Southern Cross Owners' Association, calls her a go-anywhere boat in any weather. "I feel very confident that I could take her anywhere in the world," he said. "She's a salty-looking boat that always draws looks and comments in a new harbor," he added.

Second Wind is very well-found and carries extensive instrumentation and safety equipment. "But I'd add a laptop computer, single-sideband radio, and an EPIRB for extended offshore work," he said.

As far as performance under sail goes, "she roars on a reach, but struggles upwind in light air. In 12 knots or better, she'll do 5 to 6 knots at 35 degrees apparent wind."

If the wind increases while she's sailing to windward, Bob first reefs the mainsail, then rolls up the genoa progressively. "Over 25 knots, we're down to two small headsails, or perhaps the club-footed staysail alone, and if she develops weather helm we ease the reefed main."

Under power, her two-cylinder Yanmar pushes the boat at 5.8 to 6 knots, using about half a gallon of fuel per hour. "It's noisy and bouncy, but reliable," he commented. "I think she may be a little over-propped, since I can only get up to 2,600 rpm at full throttle."

Major upgrades to *Second Wind* since her launching have been an Edson wheel and binnacle, autopilot, engine instrumentation pod on the companionway bulkhead, a Max-Prop, radar, a holding tank, a CD/FM player and a zip-on Bimini extension to the dodger." I'm planning to add a third battery and a second manual bilge pump, and I want to move the split backstay to the aft end of the hull because it's in the way of the helm."

If you're planning to buy a SC 31 for offshore work, Bob strongly advises you to have the stainless steel pintles and gudgeons on the rudder replaced with bronze

In Comparison

• Safety-at-sea factor: 7 (Rated against the 19 other boats in this book, with 1 being safest.)

• Speed rating: No sluggard. Prototype boat came third in her class in the Marion-to-Bermuda Race in 1977.

• Ocean comfort level: Two or three adults in comfort; or two adults and two kids.

ones, as he did. Also, have the deck tapped (to locate a waterlogged core and possible delamination), and check for a watertight hull-deck joint. On ocean passages, Bob suggests the SC 31 could carry a 6-gallon jerry jug of diesel on deck or in the port cockpit locker to provide 10 hours of emergency running time. You can also catch extra fresh water on deck during rain squalls, he maintains. "The SC 31 has a high toerail, and I've read where people gather rain through a freshwater fill pipe on deck."

Bob judges the accommodations to be comfortable for two people for extended offshore work, "although a third person could fit in, considering that there are two sea berths in the main cabin with lee cloths."

Conclusion

Owning a Southern Cross is like being a member of an exclusive club. There is, in fact, an owners' association with its own extensive website on the Internet (www.southern-cross.org). It maintains crew and owner lists, advertises boats and equipment for sale, and features pictures of SCs in action. The association also publishes newsletters and organizes an annual get-together in Newport, Rhode Island.

Two SC 31s were being offered for sale on the owners' website in late 1998. Hull number 85, launched in 1979, was being offered in New York state for $27,500. She had a 20-hp Yanmar engine, Aires self-steering vane gear, a dodger, various electronic instruments, and a dinghy. A sistership called *Badger*, hull number 51, was going for $33,500 down in the U.S. Virgin Islands. She had a Monitor self-steering vane gear, a 10-foot fiberglass sailing dinghy, upgraded standing rigging, and a wide range of electronics, including ham radio. There was no mention in the advertisement of what kind of engine she had.

At prices like these – less than those of many luxury cars – the SC 31 represents a bargain buy for the ocean voyager who prefers a solidly-built, highly conservative hull in the Colin Archer tradition.

Chapter Twenty
Westsail 32

She Converts Dreams to Reality

From afar, in her element, the Westsail 32 is the stuff romantic dreams are made of. Her mast is tall, her bowsprit long. A wooden tiller sweeps gracefully over a pointed stern, and a deep gunwale forms a beautifully curved sheerline that runs unbroken from the bows to just aft of the cockpit.

But as you get closer you begin to realize that there's brawn behind this beauty. The Westsail 32 is a massive boat in many ways. At 20,000 pounds displacement, 7,000 pounds of it in her keel, she is by far the biggest boat in this book. Her fittings are huge. Her decks are wide. Her topsides are high.

Compared with other boats of her vintage, going down below on a Westsail 32 is like entering a cathedral. Her 11-foot beam and 27-foot waterline was enormous for a 32-footer in the early 1970s when she was born. Here, against all the odds, was a boat big enough to swing a cat in, a mini studio apartment floating on the water, and one that could help you escape to the places you'd read about, romantic-sounding destinations such as Bora-Bora, the Galápagos, even Cape Horn itself.

The fact that the Westsail 32 could also be purchased as a kit, completed to various stages, helped fuel a frenzy of escapism in America. In the mid-1970s, demand for this boat was so great that the factory couldn't supply you with one for 18 months. Between 1971, when it all began, and 1981, when the production run ended, about 1,100 Westsail 32s were launched. Almost all are still afloat, and almost all are increasing in value.

Bud Taplin, first general manager of the builders, Westsail Corporation, figures that the increase has been 3 percent to 5 percent every year for the past five years. Talk Westsail 32, and you're talking $50,000.

"Westsail boats are one of the few lines that are worth as much now – or more, at 15 to 20 years old – as they were new during the 1970s," he claims.

Taplin is the man Westsail 32 owners turn to when they need help or advice. His Worldcruiser company offers a wide variety of services, including spare parts, instruction manuals, service manuals, and original plans. You can call him at (714) 549-9331. The brawny Westsail 32 came along at just the right time to tap into a huge pent-up demand for a solid, seaworthy boat built of maintenance-free fiberglass, and her sterling qualities have kept her in constant demand ever since.

Basic Design

The origins of the Westsail 32 are clearly Scandinavian. Bill Crealock, who had a hand in the design of the earliest models, believes the basic hull was a William Atkin design, greatly influenced by Colin Archer's larger Norwegian sea-rescue ketches of 70 years before.

In Short

Westsail 32

Designer: William Atkin/W. I. B. Crealock

LOA: 32 feet 0 inches

LWL: 27 feet 6 inches

Beam: 11 feet 0 inches

Draft: 5 feet 0 inches

Displacement: 20,000 pounds

Sail area: 663 square feet

Ballast: Encapsulated, 7,000 pounds

Spars: Aluminum

Auxiliary: Diesel

Designed as: Roomy, rugged world cruiser

Indeed, in his book *Of Yachts and Men* (Sheridan House, 1984), William Atkin features a gaff-rigged ketch called *Freya* which has the exact dimensions of the Westsail 32. *Freya* was in fact a 47-foot Colin Archer scaled down to 32 feet by Atkin, Art Hildebrand, and William Washburn Nutting, former managing editor of the magazine *Motor Boat.*

The Westsail 32 has a long, full keel with no pretense of a cutaway up forward. She's a double-ender, of course with a lifeboat stern and an outboard rudder. She's beamy and high-sided, and has a long bowsprit from which to set a lot of sail. She needs it. She's about the heaviest 32-footer afloat. The hull is solid fiberglass, laid up by hand, while the deck and the long, low cabintop are made of plywood-cored fiberglass. The first 30 or so hulls were finished with a Crealock-designed flush deck and interior, but when Snyder Vick acquired the molds in 1971 he added a trunk cabin for extra light and headroom. Almost half of the hulls produced were sold for home finishing in kit form. You'd think this would lead to a wild array of different interiors, but in fact choices were limited by the components provided, so most 32s ended up looking pretty much alike down below. The differences are mainly in the quality of the joinerwork and the quality of the fittings. Many amateur-built boats are as good as the factory-built boats, if not better, but some, naturally, fall short even of average. You can tell which boats were home-built by checking the hull identification plates. If the ID number contains the letters WSSK, the hull was sold to be finished as a kit; it if contains the letters WSSF, it was factory-finished. Incidentally, Westsail 32s were produced on both the East Coast and the West Coast. Her keel is 5 feet deep for almost the full length of the boat, which adds up to a very large underwater area of resistance. The 7,000 pounds of ballast, originally a mixture of lead pigs and steel punchings, is contained within the hull. From 1975 onward, the ballast was a solid casting of lead.

The decks are spacious, making for easy movement fore and aft, even with bulky sailbags in tow. The cockpit is tiny and exposed, little more than a footwell with 9-inch coamings on two sides, but it does have a substantial bridgedeck to separate it from the main companionway. It's an extremely seaworthy cockpit, of course, but it offers about as much comfort and protection from the elements as does a bicycle in a hailstorm. If you approve of hair coats and self-flagellation, you'll like this cockpit. If not, you'll want to invest in a large dodger.

A choice of engines was offered, the three most popular being the Volvo Penta MD 2, the Volvo MD3, and the Perkins 4-107. The MD 2 is not a good match for this boat. It's just too weak in the knees. The MD 3 has a little more muscle, but the Perkins is the

Westsail 32

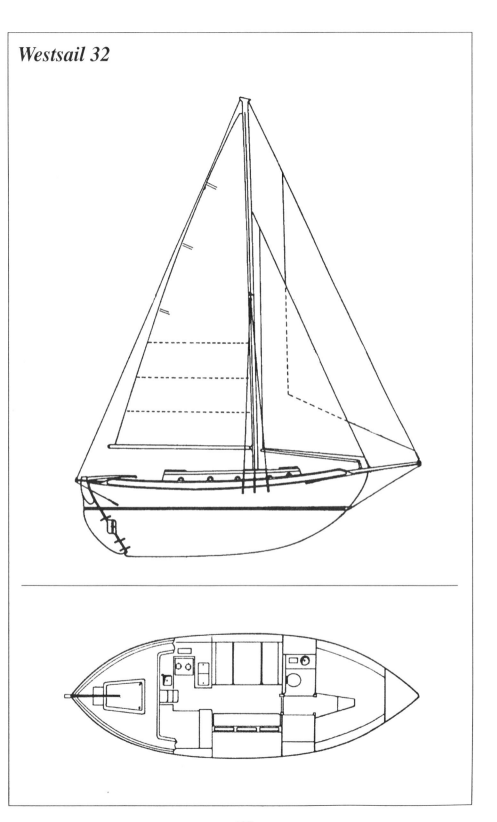

workhorse that gets the job done when the chips are down.

Accommodations

In a boat with a cavernous interior like this one, you've pretty much got room for all the necessities of life, with a few luxuries thrown in. In comparison with other boats of its length, everything down below on the Westsail 32 is huge. If you want to become a liveaboard, and can afford only a 32-footer, this is the one to choose. Just aft of the generous chain locker in the bow is a wide, very wide, V-berth. It's actually a giant double berth to port and a fat single to starboard, very suitable for a seagoing ménage á trois.

Aft of this sleeping cabin there's a bathroom to port with a hand basin and storage for linen, while to starboard there are a bureau and a hanging locker with bedding storage outboard of them.

A door in the main bulkhead leads through to the main saloon, where there are another four berths, a double to port, formed by dropping the dinette table, and a transom berth with an outboard pilot berth to starboard. All very suitable for an additional ménage á quatre, of course, except that crossing an ocean cheek-by-jowl with seven people on a 32-footer, even one of this size, is apt to spawn the wrong kind of emotions, certainly not those of the cordial type.

There's another hanging locker for wet oilskins opposite the large galley, and a proper navigation den to starboard with a chart table big enough to bring tears of joy to any navigator's eyes.

After all this profligate use of space, there's precious little room left for a cockpit, and neither (luckily) is there a quarterberth.

The Rig

The deckstepped mast and the 16-foot boom are made of aluminum, painted with linear polyurethane. Most of the masts were made by LeFiell, while others were supplied by Sparcraft, Superspar, and Royal Marine.

She's a masthead cutter with a sail area of about 630 square feet, 300 of which is in the mainsail, 150 in the staysail, and 180 in the jib.

The original rig had one forestaysail stay and one jibstay. A single backstay ended on a small boomkin outboard of the rudder head. The mast had a single set of spreaders, with a topmast shroud and sets of forward lowers and after lowers on each side. It's a strong and conservative rig, although not particularly closewinded because the shrouds, fastened to outboard chainplates at one of the beamiest parts of the hull, preclude narrow sheeting angles for the headsails. No matter, she needs the added drive anyhow.

The mainsail will normally have jiffy reefing with three reef points, and the large, fairly flat cabin top provides a roomy, stable working platform for the crew doing the reefing at the mast.

Performance

Ah yes, performance. Despite her racing successes, there are many people who give the Westsail 32 poor marks for performance. *Practical Sailor*, for example, claims "its performance is mediocre, even offshore" and adds: "It can be wet to sail and clumsy under power."

On the other hand, the Northern California PHRF rating list gives the Westsail 32 a rating of 216, which means her performance under sail is certainly nowhere near disgraceful. It gives her the same speed as Gary Mull's Ranger 23 and the Downeast 38 cutter. It makes her much faster than a Folkboat, at 234. Furthermore, Westsail 32s often surprise fellow competitors by doing very well in ocean races. One has even won the Pacific Cup outright on handicap, as we'll see under the heading Owner's Opinion.

> ### In Comparison
> - Safety-at-sea factor: 5 (Rated against the 19 other boats in this book, with 1 being safest.)
> - Speed rating: Not as slow as some people think. PHRF rating 216.
> - Ocean comfort level: Four adults in reasonable comfort.

The point here is that this hull does not reach its maximum speed quickly. She's not a fast-accelerating boat, responding quickly to every puff, so she will fare poorly on an Olympic course around the buoys. But her waterline length of 27 feet 6 inches gives her a theoretical top speed of more than 7 knots, and even if she normally reaches only 90 percent of that speed she's going to be sailing faster than most other 32-footers with shorter waterlines. That's why she does well on long passages, where it's not maximum speed that counts, but sustained high average speeds.

As for her being clumsy under power, she's only as clumsy as the person at the helm. There are ways to maneuver a heavy-displacement boat like this in confined areas but they require the skill that comes of good seamanship, practice, and familiarity with the capabilities of the boat and her engine. To describe her as clumsy is really to expose one's own limitations. This, incidentally, is not a paean in praise of the Westsail 32's maneuverability. It's merely a plea for fair play. Compared with a fin-keeler, she takes more careful handling, just as a school bus does in comparison with a family minivan. Nobody calls a school bus clumsy. Like the Westsail 32, it's just built to do a different job.

Known Weaknesses

Watch out for:

- Low-powered engines. She needs a very hefty shove against high winds and seas.
- Leaky toerails.
- Rot in the bowsprit, Sampson post, boomkin, plywood deck, and cabintop core. Check the rudder cheeks for rot also, but it's not a structural weakness because the load is taken by a metal fitting underneath.
- Osmotic blistering. Some Westsails have blistered, but usually not badly.
- Check the swaged ends on the standing rigging for hairline cracks or corrosion.
- If it hasn't been done recently, re-caulk all the deck hardware.

Owner's Opinion

David King of Portland, Oregon, has owned two Westsail 32s in a period of 23 years. He is a professional delivery skipper who also works on boats. He has had his present boat, *Saraband*, for 11 years.

In 1988, in *Saraband*, he won the prestigious Pacific Cup race from San Francisco to Oahu, Hawaii. *Saraband*, a stock Westsail 32, came first in class and won first place overall on handicap. Naturally, there was an uproar, especially among the owners of larger racing boats commissioned at huge expense and carrying trained racing crews. There was not a single racer in *Saraband*'s crew of five, although all were experienced cruisers.

In 1990, King decided it was his duty to show the racing world that the Westsail 32's success had not been a one-time fluke. He entered Saraband for the Pacific Cup again, and this time she was first in her class to finish, and first in her class on handicap. She came third overall on handicap.

Three protests were handed in, and all three failed. One protest charged that *Saraband*'s spinnaker was too large. When it was measured it was found to be a 168 percent spinnaker, rather than the 180 percent spinnaker the rules allowed.

What was the secret of *Saraband*'s success?

"Most Westsails suffer from having to drag a big three-bladed propeller through the water," King said. "We have a Max-Prop automatic feathering propeller and it makes a big difference. *Saraband* gets up to 7 knots pretty quickly."

She sustains her speed well, too. She has sailed more than 180 miles in 24 hours in three occasions, two while racing and one during a singlehanded passage. "I did 184 miles all by myself one day," he said.

Saraband experiences a little weather helm as she heels over, "but it's never excessive," he added. "She's always under control."

If the wind rises while his cutter's on a beat, the first action King takes is to reduce the size of the genoa jib. "I reef it down to the size of a working jib," he explained. "The next step, if the wind continues to rise, is to tuck a reef into the mainsail. Next in order is a second reef in the main, after which I'd drop the jib completely. Now, under double-reefed main and working staysail, she's good for 40-knots-plus."

Westsails are often criticized for not being able to beat.

"That's a huge exaggeration," King said. "It's just not so. She goes to windward at the speed of a 29-foot or 30-foot boat. OK, that's not so good because she's a 32-footer, but it's not terribly bad either because most 30-footers are half her displacement and don't have her comfort or seaworthiness." King and his wife once sailed *Saraband* from Palmyra to Hawaii, a passage of about 1,000 miles, in "reinforced trades," and averaged 110 miles a day on a hard beat.

"Compared with other boats, she goes best on a close reach," he said. "In fact it's very interesting that she goes from her comparative worst (the beat) to her comparative best (the close reach) in a matter of a few degrees."

King said he couldn't recall his boats having any structural problems. "Nothing stands out. I did know of one boat where the mast compression post tended to impale the cabin top, but Bud Taplin worked out a quick and easy solution by fastening bolts through the coaming to the main bulkhead."

Conclusion

This is a serious world cruiser, a rugged example of a traditional design that excelled in everyday conditions in Northern European waters in the days of sailing workboats. She is roomy, exceptionally so for a 32-footer, and performs safely and adequately, sometimes brilliantly.

At $50,000 she is not the cheapest used 32-footer around (nor, by a long chalk, the most expensive) but she does offer good value for money and – significantly – seems to maintain that value indefinitely. There are times when boat values rise and fall en bloc – witness the sudden plunge of the early 1990s, for example – but the Westsail always appears to bounce back.

A few people, particularly singlehanders, might find this boat a little bulky sometimes, a lot of hard work for one person to handle and maintain, but most adventurers have no need to be intimidated by her size, which shrinks with familiarity. There is no sign, even after nearly three decades, that the Westsail 32's strong appeal to would-be world cruisers will wane any time soon.

Bibliography

Casey, Don. *This Old Boat.* Camden, ME: International Marine, 1990.

Gerr, Dave. *The Nature of Boats.* Camden, ME: International Marine, 1992.

Gustafson, Charles. *How to Buy the Best Sailboat.* New York: Hearst Marine Books, 1985.

Henderson, Richard. *Singlehanded Sailing.* Second Edition. Camden, ME: International Marine, 1988.

Herreshoff, L. Francis. *Sensible Cruising Designs.* Camden, ME: International Marine, 1991.

Hiscock, Eric C. *Cruising Under Sail.* Third Edition. Camden, ME: International Marine, 1981.

Hiscock, Eric C. *Voyaging Under Sail.* Second Edition. Camden, ME: International Marine, 1981.

Kinney, Francis S. *Skene's Elements of Yacht Design.* Eighth Edition. New York: Dodd, Mead & Co., 1981.

Marchaj, C. A. *Seaworthiness, The Forgotten Factor.* Camden. ME: International Marine, 1987.

Marrett, Barbara, and John Neal. *Mahina Tiare, Pacific Passages.* Friday Harbor, WA: Pacific International Publishing Company, 1993.

Neal, John. *Log of the Mahina.* Friday Harbor, WA: Pacific International Publishing Company: 1993.

Pardey, Lin and Larry. *The Capable Cruiser.* Paradise Cay Publications, P.O. Box 29, Arcata, CA 95518-0029, 800-736-4509. www.paracay.com.

Pardey, Lin and Larry. *The Self-Sufficient Sailor.* Paradise Cay Publications, P.O. Box 29, Arcata, CA 95518-0029, 800-736-4509. www.paracay.com.

Pardey, Lin and Larry. *The Cost-Conscious Cruiser.* Paradise Cay Publications, P.O. Box 29, Arcata, CA 95518-0029, 800-736-4509. www.paracay.com.

Spurr, Dan. *Spurr's Boat Book: Upgrading the Cruising Sailboat.* Camden, ME: International Marine, 1983.

Vigor, John. *Danger, Dolphins & Ginger Beer.* New York: Atheneum, 1993.

Vigor, John. *The Practical Mariner's Book of Knowledge.* Camden, ME: International Marine, 1994.

Vigor, John. *The Sailor's Assistant.* Camden, ME: International Marine, 1997.

Vigor, John. *The Seaworthy Offshore Sailboat.* Camden, ME: International Marine, 1999.

White, E. B. "The Sea and the Wind That Blows," published in *Essays of E. B. White.* New York: Harper-Collins Publishers, 1963.

More Books from Paradise Cay Publications...

COST CONSCIOUS CRUISER

by Lin and Larry Pardey,
In this book Lin & Larry discuss topics ranging from making your getaway plans to finding a truly affordable boat, keeping your outfitting costs and maintenance time in control, then learning to feel confident as you cruise farther ahead.

Their chart of the gear considered necessary by many shoreside experts, compared to that carried by several cost-conscious cruisers, will give you a convenient checklist to gauge whether you are buying true necessities or overloading your budget and boat with high-tech items that can break down and steal your sense of confidence offshore.

THE CAPABLE CRUISER

by Lin & Larry Pardey
A Dolphin Book Club "Main Selection," The Capable Cruiser illustrates how successful cruising is the result of a combination of factors including a homogeneous crew, proper preparation, solid gear, regular maintenance and exemplary seamanship. This book is the sequel to The Self Sufficient Sailor. This is indeed the global bible of cruising sailors.

CARE AND FEEDING OF SAILING CREW

by Lin & Larry Pardey
Expanded by more than 30%, this book tells not only how to buy, provision and stow food for local cruising and extended voyages, but also how to take care of all the other aspects of crew comfort. Sleep, outfitting

galleys, keeping warm and dry, medical considerations, building an efficiently insulated freezer/fridge/ice chest, water and watermakers plus one of the most innovative gimbaled stoves afloat.

CRUISING IN SERAFFYN

by Lin & Larry Pardey
This cruising tale is full of the sights and sounds, the fragrances and native customs of foreign lands, especially Central America and the Caribbean.

DETAILS OF CLASSIC BOAT CONSTRUCTION: THE HULL

by Larry Pardey
Building a wooden hull is discussed in detail, step-by-step with illustrations including 600 photographs and 178 diagrams, vital information for potential builders, repair specialists, designers and owners of wooden hulls.

SERAFFYN'S EUROPEAN ADVENTURE

by Lin & Larry Pardey
Join Lin and Larry while they winter in England working to pay for the next leg of their journey into the Baltic, Denmark, Sweden, Finland, Germany. They dealt with armed guards on the Polish waterfront who watched while the people greeted them with flowers and fruit. They weathered a fierce mast-under broach in a Baltic gale.

SERAFFYN'S MEDITERRANEAN ADVENTURE

by Lin & Larry Pardey
Lin and Larry Pardey spent 11 years cruising the world in their backyard-built, 24-foot

cutter Seraffyn. Seraffyn's Mediterranean Adventure covers three years of their cruising life, in and around the Mediterranean, where they explored the Spanish Coast and then worked their way back down to the African coast and the Arab world.

THE CHINESE SAILING RIG: DESIGNING & BUILDING YOUR OWN

by Derek Van Loan with Dan Haggerty
The Chinese Sailing Rig - Designing and Building Your Own is a practical handbook which emphasizes adapting western hulls to a Chinese rig. Its "take a hammer in one hand and a nail in the other" approach leads the amateur designer/builder through all the steps from dream to voyage. The emphasis here is on "practical."

CRUISING CHEF COOKBOOK 2ND EDITION

by Michael Greenwald
The new Cruising Chef is actually a book of nautical wisdom in the guise of a cookbook. It contains hundreds of tips plus more than 300 delicious recipes. Includes an extensive discussion of preparing for a voyage and resupplying in native markets.

A CRUISING GUIDE FROM ACAPULCO TO THE PANAMA CANAL

by Charles & Nancy Goodman
The passage between Acapulco and the Panama Canal offers some of the best and some of the least known cruising areas in the world. In early 1988 a group of

"yachties" gathered for a meeting at the Acapulco Yacht Club to compare notes, ideas and personal information about the trip to the canal. This cruising guide contains detailed descriptions of 51 Anchorages between Acapulco and the Panama Canal.

CRUISING GUIDE TO THE HAWAIIAN ISLANDS

by Bob and Carolyn Mehaffy Paperback
In this new *Cruising Guide to the Hawaiian Islands,* boaters will find the most comprehensive guide to the Hawaiian Islands ever published, with detailed coverage of 68 harbors and anchorages in the Islands, including Midway Atoll. *Cruising Guide to the Hawaiian Islands* is an essential companion for all boaters who plan to cruise in the Hawaiian Islands, whether by powerboat or by sailboat.

CRUISING GUIDE TO SAN FRANCISCO BAY, 2ND EDITION

by Bob & Carolyn Mehaffy
In this updated and expanded second edition, this comprehensive cruising guide includes four more destinations outside the Bay: Pillar Point Harbor, Drakes Bay, Bodega Harbor, and Tomales Bay. For the more than 70 destinations covered, the authors give detailed instructions on how to get there safely, where to anchor or tie up, and what to do there.

THE CHINESE SAILING RIG: DESIGNING AND BUILDING YOUR OWN

by Derek Van Loan
A practical handbook for sailors wishing to adapt the junk rig to western style hulls.

Emphasis is on practical, straightforward design and construction choices with tested materials and methods throughout. Includes instructions on sailing the rig.

BREATHTAKING – ONE MAN, ONE WOMAN, ONE BOAT:TWO HAPPY DAYS

by J.P. Valdury
Nick knew better than to buy a boat, but that didn't stop him. He bought a boat because Claire-Anne wanted it, needed it, dreamed about it, went electric with excitement when she talked about it... And Claire-Anne was very beautiful when she was excited.
A good humored romp.

ON THE BOULEVARD OF GALLEONS

by Wallace B. Farrell & Sandra J. Burns
On the Boulevard of Galleons is the account of a two-year sailing adventure retracing the paths of Spanish treasure ships and buccaneers in the New World. The voyage sweeps along the stark Bala peninsula and down the unspoiled Gold Coast to Acapulco.

SPRING TIDES

by Ed Larson
Spring Tides is more than a story of boats and the sea. It speaks of the adventure and beauty of Alaska in an era when boats were made of wood and the world seemed a more sane and simple place. There is death in the pages and the drama and triumph of survival - best of all, everything really happened.

SURVIVOR

by Michael Greenwald
Required reading for all sailors! Caught in the eye of the hurricane, sudden

disaster in the night, attacked by killer whales, shipwrecked in the dead of winter on an Alaskan island: these are a few of the many adventures described in *Survivor,* a boat disaster anthology so gripping you won't be able to put it down. True stories of the struggle for life in tiny survival craft, or cast up on an uninhabited coral atoll, stark photos of castaways, daring rescues, tragic failures, and a wealth of solid survival lore make *Survivor* a sailor's manual, required reading for those who go to sea.

TAKING TERRAPIN HOME:A LOVE AFFAIR WITH A SMALL CATAMARAN

by Mathew Wilson
An exciting account of crossing the Atlantic in a small sailboat by Mathew Wilson, a noted lecturer who used his adventure as the subject for this, his first book. *Terrapin's* route took her across the English Channel, through France to the Mediterranean before turning to cross the Atlantic. There are no heroics. This is not a survival manual. This is a good story.

100 PROBLEMS IN CELESTIAL NAVIGATION

by Leonard Cray
Noted author Leonard Gray treats us again with this potpourri of celestial navigation exercises, each designed around a specific journey; New York to Lisbon, Anchorage to Hilo, Hungnam to Akita to name a few.
Each voyage (19 in all) presents not only realistic celestial observation data, but also other considerations germane to the type of voyage.

THE COMPASS BOOK

by Mike Harris

The magnetic compass is one of the most ancient of navigational instruments, and even in these times, it remains a vital piece of gear for any boat.

The Compass Book is an introduction to the principles of compass work. It is a guide for those wanting to carry out as much of their own repair and maintenance work as possible.

GPS MADE EASY, 2ND EDITION

by Lawrence Letham

Completely revised. All you need to know about using hand-held GPS receivers as a tool for accurate navigation in the outdoors. Written for both land and water use.

NAUTICAL ALMANAC

Edited by Matt Morehouse

Commercial Edition. This is the cornerstone for all sight reduction. The *Nautical Almanac* lists the positions of the sun, moon, stars, and planets that are used for navigation. It also contains a short version of a sight reduction table that may be used in an emergency.

NAVIGATION RULES (RULES OF THE ROAD)

Required on board all vessels 12 meters or more in length. *Navigation Rules* is one of the items a Coast Guard boarding officer will ask for during a routine "safety" inspection. The rules are presented in a convenient format emphasizing distinctions between inland and international rules.

THE STAR FINDER BOOK

by David Burch,

A comprehensive book explaining the use of the 2102D star finder, and the many applications it offers in planning navigation. Its numerous examples and diagrams make it a most definitive treatment. This book is an indispensable companion to the star finder itself.

DRUG TESTING

by Captain Alan Spears Esq.

Captain Spears examines the procedures prescribed in 46 CFR Part 16 and 49 CFR Part 40 as they pertain to the collection of drug test specimens from licensed mariners. Drug testing explains random, reasonable cause, and pre-employment testing procedures; analyzes legal cases; and discusses employer-generated pre-termination (discharge) hearings.

HOW TO SURVIVE WITH A POWERSURVIVOR WATERMAKER

by Gary E. Albers aboard S/V ISHI

Here is a source of accurate and reliable information on how to choose, install, maintain and rebuild the popular PÚR PowerSurvivor watermakers manufactured by Recovery Engineering, Inc. Included are detailed, illustrated chapters on the disassembly and repair of the new Endurance models of watermakers from PUR, as well as the ubiquitous PowerSurvivor 35.

LANDFALL LEGALESE - VOLUME I: THE PACIFIC

Captain Alan Spears, Esq.

VOLUME II: THE CARIB-BEAN

Captain Alan Spears, Esq.

If you are going cruising in the Pacific or the Caribbean, and you are interested in previewing the required customs and immigration forms prior to arrival, *Landfall Legalese* is a must. Together, Volumes I and II comprise a compendium of the legal requirements and protocols for entering and clearing the majority of popular cruising ports throughout the Pacific and the Caribbean.

SHIPPING OUT

by Captain Alan Spears, Esq.

An exposé of commercial and recreational shipboard jobs. A practical reference for job-seeking mariners describing various methods of finding work in the industry.

DRAG DEVICE DATA BASE

by Victor Shane

Over 120 documented case histories, involving both power and sail, pleasure and commercial vessels, of effective use at sea of parachutes, sea anchors and drogues to cope with heavy weather. Many clear diagrams, photos.

STORM TACTICS HANDBOOK: MODERN METHODS OF HEAVING-TO FOR SURVIVAL IN EXTREME CONDITIONS

by Lin & Larry Pardey

Modern methods of heaving-to for survival in extreme conditions. Trysail and para-anchor technology for all types of boats and sailors.

For a free Paradise Cay Publications catalog, call 1-800-736-4509, or visit our web site at www.paracay.com